TROPICAL FISH

setting up and maintaining freshwater and marine aquaria

TROPICAL FISH

setting up and maintaining freshwater and marine aquaria

by Reginald Dutta

Foreword by Robert A. Morris
Former Curator, New York Aquarium
(New York Zoological Society)

Photographs by
Moorfield Aquatics

derbibooks

Endpapers: Capoeta arulius.
5". Largish, peaceful. Fast mid-water
swimmer. Needs plenty of room.
Likes plants.

Top left: Anostomus trimaculatus.
8". Guyana. Another big beauty,
peaceful for its size. Prominent black
dots, pleasant green sheened body.
Eats green foods.
Centre left: Toxotes jaculator.
Archer Fish. 6" Malaysia.
Dark, smudgy colours denote turbid or
brackish waters. The mouth enables it
to cruise just below the surface.
It shoots down its prey with water
pellets.

Top right: Barbodes lateristriga.
The 'minus eleven' Barb, or Spanner
Barb of old. 6". Malaysia.
Typical Barb silver grey sheened body,
with markings. Peaceful and slow –
almost a stay-at-home.

Centre right: Rasbora caudimaculata.
Giant Scissortail. 8". Malaysia.
Nicely balanced. Striking yellow and
black markings on tail lobes.
Needs clean clear bright waters with
space to roam.

Frontispiece: Malapterurus
electricus. *The famous electric eel that*
stings for defence. Not for a community
tank. Large.
Overleaf: *Malayan barbs: playful,*
like most of their kind; grow large;
peaceful.

First published in paperback in the
United States of America 1975 by
Derbibooks and distributed by
Book Sales Inc., 110 Enterprise Avenue
Secaucus, N.J. 07094

© 1972 Octopus Books Limited

ISBN 0 7064 0489 0

Produced by Mandarin Publishers Limited
Toppan Building, Westlands Road, Quarry Bay,
Hong Kong

Printed in Hong Kong

Foreword by ROBERT A. MORRIS

Former Curator, New York Aquarium
(New York Zoological Society)

Man has plundered his environment both above ground and under-water. As he seeks to understand the complex relationships that exist between the multitude of plants and animals, he turns more and more to other sources.

The home aquarist and fish keeper has long been aware of the complex problems of crowding and pollution. Many different species of fish must be kept together harmoniously in an artificial environment. A home must be constructed, plants placed in the proper perspective and the water medium added. The problems have just begun. What fish live well together? How can water be purified and reused over and over again? The problems seem as insurmountable as those facing our environment today.

Despite these difficulties the hobby has grown rapidly. It now has expanded into the exciting and even more complex realm of maintaining ocean life. As our knowledge of keeping and maintaining aquarium life grows, so must we share this knowledge with fellow man. Who knows – perhaps methods of water cleansing developed by some hobbyist may someday be applied on a much grander scale to purify the polluted waters of our environment. Perhaps a new tropical fish food may allow the expansion of giant fish farms to feed starving populations.

Reginald Dutta has shared his valuable experiences in fish keeping with you in **Tropical Fish**. Excellent photographs, as well as new ideas on aquarium management, furnish the necessary information for the beginning and experienced hobbyist alike.

CONTENTS

CHAPTER 1
AQUARIUM

To your pet fish the aquarium is its entire home, a place it will never leave, twenty-four hours for each and every relentlessly unchanging day, for the rest of its whole life. Please make the home a nice one!

Fortunately your choice is enormous, as this fast growing industry ever pours out new and improved models in shapes, sizes, colours and materials that will leave you breathless with delight, and gratified at the low price. The demand has called forth a world wide supply – after all, whether we live in America, Australia, Canada, England or whatever, hot climate or cold, our changed way of life has forced the growth of the aquarium industry.

In the old days, our grandfathers often lived in spacious surroundings and kept horses or cattle; our parents lived tighter packed in cities but still managed to keep dogs and cats; but you and I survive boxed up in an apartment, be it luxury or poor it lacks space – you couldn't really live with a horse in there too, nor a dog that will bark and disturb the neighbours, or mess the carpet if you're late coming home, and so we keep tropical fish. They don't bark, make puddles, can be left without feeding while we're away at work or holiday, take up tiny spaces and don't need to be taken out for exercise. Add to that their beauty, the sheer thrill of fabulous colours, quaint and graceful shapes, the flow of the trailing fins, the personal characteristics they develop and display to our joy or annoyance, the way they get tame, come when we call, beg for food and flatter our ego with the pure unrestrained pleasure at seeing us approach their tank.

Any human who says that fish have no feelings has got a lot to learn – and, given a chance, the fish will soon teach him. No wonder they're popular, and the demand for them has grown right round the world.

Golden rule So, what sort of tank are you going to buy? First, it must be big enough; that is, have as big an air surface as possible to let the oxygen in and the bad gasses out. Height from top to bottom is merely to please you; length, and width, from back to front, is vital for fish health – and it's their home, not yours. Modern power filters are a real help in overcoming difficulties of restricted oxygenation but the above *golden rule* always applies, and woe to the human who disregards it – the air surface *must* be big enough!

Lightweights Cheap and popular, their tendency to leak has been overcome by the new adhesive sealers; these come in tubes, **11**

Above: Hemigrammus ocellifer. *The Beacon Fish, the Motorist Fish, the Head and Tail Light.* 2″. *Amazon. Luminous dots, clear sheened body. Hates cold, and then gets white spot, but recovers quickly. Male is smaller and slimmer.* 75°–80°F (24°–27°C).
Extreme left: Nannostomus anomalus. *One of the many 'Pencil' fish.* 2″. *River Negro. With its defensive colouring, dainty mouth, and small size it needs protective thickets and clean waters. Shy, likes to be in shoals. Likes green foods.* 75°–82°F (24°–28°C) *pH 6·8, DH 4.*
Left: Hyphessobrycon pulchripinnis. *Lemon Tetra.* 2″. *Amazon. Named after the striking bright yellow tips of its dorsal and anal fins. Gregarious.* 74°–78°F (23°–26°C), *pH 7, DH 6–8.*

rather like toothpaste, and are best nozzled out 'uphill', i.e. away from you as you work along the inside joints making sure that no gaps are left.

Angle-iron frames These are the more robust angle-iron framed tanks, that everyone knows and loves. The new polythene or nylon coatings for the metal have solved the problem of rust, and have made them safe for use with marines. The coatings come in many lovely colours, with white and black being most in demand.

Special metals The Americans with stainless steel, and the Germans with anodized aluminium, are leading the field but with limited success. The magic description 'rustless' has lost its power in the face of the far cheaper nylon coatings; and the system of slotting or clipping together the corners (instead of welding) leaves a weakness that is not entirely eliminated by the (messy) black bostic-type of sealing compound normally used. Yet, these metals do give a beautiful finish.

Tall tanks Increased height means increased water pressure all round so that expense rockets; now the new rubber adhesives maintain waterproofing without the necessity of wide angle-iron which is ugly, costly and heavy. Hence the surge in popularity of the taller models, often incorporating toughened or armoured glass.

All-glass tanks Wonderful new 'glues' will now stick glass direct to glass with a 'purchase' or surface contact of only $\frac{1}{4}''$. It sounds incredible to be able to join two long pieces of glass only $\frac{1}{4}''$ thick, edge to edge, and angled at that. Tanks 4 feet long or more, with sloping fronts, are now commonplace. Only the degree of expansion and contraction of the glass itself under temperature variation now hinders size; the problem of water pressure has been completely overcome as far as the bonding is concerned.

Thus has started a whole new generation of tanks, completely rustless and non-toxic, ideal for marines. The 'ugly' (because it is robust) metal support frame has been entirely eliminated, and side trimmings can now be for beauty only, not function; of a delicacy, fragility, grace, separated or spaced charm hitherto quite impossible. They can be made of formerly unusable materials like wafer-thin metals or plastics or woods or threads or beads or filigree work, or whatever can be joined, blended and interweaved.

The way for artistic beauty is wide wide open. Not only glass joined to glass, but to wood, to plastic; pliable, rigid; fluted, curved; coloured, opaque, translucent; many sided, circular, half-moon; so many lovely choices for the specialist and the skilled. We love doing a 'one-off' job exactly for that spot in that room in that décor. As manufacturers tool up, these gorgeous lines pour off the production benches at absurdly cheap prices, in ever changing models.

Plastic tanks Particularly active in producing new designs is the plastic injection-moulded factory. Technical breakthroughs at the end of the 1960s enabled very deep tanks to be moulded in one piece; add to that the infinite variation of colour, of shape, or curve, and even of height (a big stumbling block before) and

Above: Hyphessobrycon herbertaxelrodi. *Black Neon. 1¾". River Negro. Named after the longitudinal black bar with green upper edge. Very attractive in strong, oblique light. Shy, but lovely in small planted tanks and in shoals. DH 4–8.*

Above right : Hyphessobrycon serpae.
*1¾". Amazon. Stronger coloured than
the* H. ornatus, *but smaller and
without the striking dorsal fin.
Standard preferences.*

the rustless, non-toxic tank has charmed its way into thousands
of homes.

Light 'travels' through plastic to give beautiful hues, ever
changing with angle, with intensity, and with distance to focus
a real advantage over obsolescent materials; people who are
still moaning about plastic scratching and discolouring just
haven't caught up.

Specialities Pirating of designs is not limited to Paris cou-
turiers or to motorcars. Our 'New Age' model was gently curved
left to right, and top to bottom, was Zeppelin-shaped and trimmed with contrasting twisted plastic strips down which the toplighting sent flowing jets of light; the whole was mounted on
crystal clear legs, almost invisible, to give the wonderful impression of a space ship in flight. Internally, air bubbles danced,
spotlights featured chosen motifs, and the fish glided serenely
through light and shade. No wonder the pirates grabbed!

Why limit originality of creation to one tank?

Take a corner; façade and re-shape it into a replica of an old
pioneer wagon of American Wild West days, or the old stage
coach; tanks being windows, sloped or angled sides, roofs, sup-
ports, broken wheels, etc, etc.

Take a wall; tier it with large and small tanks, round, square
and tall; in patterns and rhythm; diamond-like, V-shaped,
hoops or arrows; tiny Maculata or Cardinals in tiny tanks
clustering round a huge eye-catcher; alternately brightly and
darkly lit; modern, futuristic, traditional décor alternating tank
by tank. You'd never get your friends to leave it!

Take a conservatory, full of flowers. Add these tall, fluted
vase-like tanks, soaring on graceful slender wood columns; have
a pool, not sunk static in the floor, but new-type raised on a
stand so that the fish are at your height, where you can talk to **13**

them, see them, make friends with them, hand feed them, tickle them, let them snuggle in your cupped hand; add the soft sound of falling water to gentle lighting. What a cure for headaches, insomnia or worry.

All is now possible in this jet age. Nowhere on the planet is more than a few hours away. Experts travel, international clientèles grow; that soon translates into mass production, and into so many happy homes. No wonder people love tropical fish.

How about a tank on your yacht; for decorative or for edible fish? Long since passed are the days when the pitch and roll of the ship made things too difficult; many an ocean liner has them in the stateroom.

Tank lighting A wonderful help in the creation of beauty, tank lighting should give an all-over even spread to enable all the plants to thrive. Incandescent bulbs of 25 watts per square foot of water surface, housed 3″ above, for eight hours per day is normal; excess light causes green algae; insufficient light makes the plants wilt. The new 'Gro-Lux' from America is rapidly displacing all other types because it heightens the colours (especially the blues, reds and greens) by removing the yellowish caste.

Speciality lighting Creative beauty demands more than a top light plonked on top, with and without feed hole.

Ever had a headache? Try the restful peace, the meditative quiet, of a nicely arranged aquascape with no top lighting at all but with very very gently diffused rear lighting, exterior to the tank, shining softly through the sides and/or back from the far far distance. In the evening, when dusk changes to dark, and if you're alone and relaxing, it can be lovely. Of course the whole effect dissipates if some clot bangs the door and slams on the room lights.

Colour is pleasant too; a blue, a green, an orange bulb works wonders; according to your mood. Often we incorporate a time switch so that three choices follow in sequence – two different

14 colours and a plain; two bursts and a pause of darkness; two

Left: Hemigrammus caudovittatus. *Buenos Aires Tetra. 4″. Big. Can well look after itself. Female can kill the male if he does not leave (or if you do not remove him) after spawning. She will also attack any male too weak or not ready to spawn. Heavy eaters.*
Right: Thayeria boehlki. *3½″. Amazon basin. Gregarious. Can snap when irritated or alone. Best in a shoal in bright waters.*
Bottom right: Pristella riddlei. *2″. Venezuela. Often called the X-Ray Tetra from its clear body by the fins, which are black-tipped and gold-rimmed. Peaceful, gregarious. Firm favourite.*

diffused and one intensely focused to light up a particular motif, or a dance of bubbles, or a moving water wheel, or a prize palm-like plant waving gently in response to the inlet pipe of the filter as it steadily pours in. Combine it with sound as you raise the inlet pipe and let the water fall from a discreet height, not too obtrusive, perhaps even in a fine spray if your filter can rise to such subtleties.

For a gay evening, for a cocktail bar, for a real hearty extro-vert affair; alternate your bright top lighting with an external frontal triple-choice time switch – a flood of colour to swamp not just the tank and cover, but part of the surrounding room as well; next one (or multiple) penetrating beams of light, rapier-like, flashing through the tank, right through. The pause of darkness, and arresting reappearance can be dramatic, so too can changing colours. For a big lush restaurant we incorporated both these themes in a 'jungle setting'. First the backcloth shaded from dawn, sunrise, noon, sunset, to darkness; in se-quence there were jungle noises lashed with a rainstorm for good

Below: Abramites microcephalus. *Marbled Headstander.* *5″. Amazon. A curious mixture of a terminal (forward pointing) mouth and a downward slanting body.* *Stands any waters, even murky ones.* *Eats anything. Peaceful.* *Dislikes temperatures lower than 75°F (24°C).*

Characics

Above: Hemigrammus rhodostomus.
2". *Brazil. Note its lovely red nose, and
scissor tail. Male is larger and slimmer.
Americans and Australians call it
Rummy Nose. 74°–80°F (23°–27°C),
pH 6·8, DH 6–8.*
Left: Hemigrammus pulcher. 2".
*Peru. A well-known version of the
Beacon Fish with its head and tail light.
Note the more striking tail markings,
and that the rear colouration is more
widespread, extending in breeding
condition even into the tail and anal fins.
Fry hatch in the usual 24–36 hours, and
are free swimming in 3 days. 75°–80°F
(24°–27°C), pH 6·8, DH 6–8.* **17**

Left : Hyphessobrycon rubrostigma.
The famous Bleeding Heart Tetra. 3″.
Clear sheened body, bright red eye,
magnificent dorsal gold tinged on top,
and blue sheened anal.
Standard preferences for the upper
Amazon types ; clean, clear, soft, aerated,
warm waters, well shaded above.
Below : Hyphessobrycon innesi.
Neon Tetra. 1¾″. Amazon.
This fabulous fish has gleaming red
and green/blue stripes shining from
within-out ; easily distinguished from
the larger and even more vivid Cardinal
because the irridescent red line does not
quite extend into the tail. It breeds easily
in clean, aerated waters. 75°–80°F
(24°–27°C), pH 6·8, DH 2–4.
Right and overleaf : Cheirodon
axelrodi. *The Cardinal Tetra. 2¾″.*
From the River Negro in Brazil.
The most beautiful of them all.
The magnificently vivid within-out
gleaming red goes right to the caudal
peduncle. Breeding, sexing, and conditions
as for the Neon.

Left: Metynnis schreitmulleri.
8″. *Amazon. Large and round.
Usually silver sheen, but breeding
colours are yellow/green tinge, with
darker back. Tough mouth, tough
fish. Eats anything, always
hungry, but not unduly pugnacious.*
Right: Carnegiella strigata.
Hatchet Fish. 2″. *Smaller and
rarer than C.* Sternicla, *but
preferences similar. Graceful top
swimmers as denoted by their
supra-terminal mouths and huge
pectoral fins that enable them to
jump fast and far. As you would
expect, they are accustomed to real
warmth, 78°–82°F (26°–28°C)
and hate cold draughts, which
brings on white spot disease.
Otherwise hardy. Please keep the
water surface free of scum, and
feed from the top.*

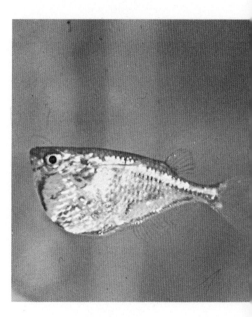

Serrasalmo nattereri. *The famous
Red Piranha from the Amazon growing
to an imposing 11". Hair-raising stories
are told of people being eaten alive by
shoals of these fish; in the aquarium the
few isolated specimens are far more
likely to be scared of your hand!
Carnivore; not to be kept with other
fish! Gets very attracted by blood or the
smell thereof. Can swim fast and far,
and can jump. Clear, aerated, open
waters suit them.*

measure. The combination of colour, mood, sound and rain was fabulous, and the (large) fish loved it, showing off and flashing their fins fit to please the toughest and the loudest.

Tank stands Tanks are heavy, a gallon of water weighs 10 lb. and fish are best seen at eye-level; 36″ off ground for the *base* of the tank for sitting eye-level, or 48″ up if you are standing. All that stuff about 'my furniture is modern and I want it low' merely results in your looking down on the (unattractive) top light, losing the beauty of the fish, having to stoop, and paying osteopath's fees to cure your slipped disc.

Multiplying length $\times$ width $\times$ height (in feet) $\times$ $6\frac{1}{4}$ gives the (English) gallons your tank holds (1 Imperial gallon$=4\cdot5459$ litres$=0\cdot1605$ cubic feet; 1 United States gallon$=3\cdot785$ litres$=0\cdot1339$ cubic feet), so you need a strongish stand. These are widely sold, often in knock-down form, and often including a second tank on the lower shelf to the intense delight of osteopaths.

Ever tried hanging a tank from the ceiling? The effect can be superb; a steadying arm to some rigid anchor, to prevent swaying as your guests coo round, would help; the chains can be chrome, sheathed in cloth, threaded with colour or beads; baubles and/or motifs can be hung from them; plain or fussy, they can be fun.

Ever tried a multiple stand of a parent column of fluted wood tapering to a dramatic top, flanked by two smaller daughter columns holding additional tanks or ornaments, photographs, lights, etc? Suitable (strong) wooden platforms floating atop the columns and fitted snugly and evenly over the tank base can be an asset rather than merely functional.

What's wrong with wall brackets (several if necessary) with a nice formica top holding the tank? Or a bookcase, incorporating subsidiary lights and shelves for flowers?

The golden rule is to give the base an all-over support; overlapping tank parts are liable to strain and hence to leak. Further, although the tank is heavy the weight is 'static' and evenly distributed – so you don't have to construct a monstrosity that would carry the weight several times over. Neat little refinements like wall-plugging parts that might sway are usually enough. A small kink in the legs of the stand to match the skirting board enables you to keep the tank flush to the wall – giving greater support and greater access to a retaining clip housed on the wall in case young children tug at the front.

If increased stability is important the legs of the stand can be splayed outwards if you have plenty of room in front, or sideways if you are somewhat cramped.

Tank position Incidentally, where are you going to position the tank? If you think you'll only potter over to it now and again for the odd glance or two, you're in for a surprise. The tank will dominate and fascinate you, and by the time you've changed from one tired leg to another, stooped and stretched the like of which you haven't done since school physical training, lugged the chair back and forth, paid yet more osteopath fees; you'll finally decide to stop and rearrange the room to suit the tank. Alternatively, you can think about it now.

If to be viewed from a distance – say of six to ten feet – the tank should be biggish, so should the fish, and the top lighting relatively diffused. The décor inside should be of broad sweep, rather than of detail (see chapter 5).

If to be viewed close to, then the entire scale can be smaller, and finesse of detail inside the tank will take precedence. Lighting can be far more focused, and attention will tend to stay on the inside, rather than on the total tank, its framework, and the room area around it.

By the way, where's your window – and the sunlight? Too much light and your tank will tend to go green. Some advise that you should allow sunlight to reach your tank for an hour or so per day; such people are usually interested solely in the fish and mutter that a (beautiful) décor detracts from them. Those who prefer overall total beauty including décor, fish and ambient room surroundings realize that sunlight cannot easily be controlled and place the tank in a protected site where (a) the artificial lighting shows up best, as in winter evenings, and (b) the growth of algae can be easily regulated.

If, for instance, the tank abuts on to a window where the outside temperature fluctuates with the seasons, then some insulation at the rear would be sensible. Polystyrene ceiling tiles can easily be stuck on to the exterior of the rear glass; so too can ornamental backgrounds, or papers. For really effective insulation the rear of the tank should be overlapped both in height and in length.

If the tank is to be sited near the kitchen or bathroom, where smells and grease will tend to foul the water, then particular attention must be paid to (stronger) filters. Excess tobacco smoke, for instance, would also need consideration.

All these problems can easily be overcome, but they are mentioned here in case you have a choice of sites. For the record we have kept tanks in crowded bars and exhibitions, in conditions where the human staff have wilted and groaned, but the fish have gone merrily on year after year – without any filters at all.

Above left: Astynax jordani. *Blind Cave. 3½″. San Luis Potosi, Mexico. A normal fish elsewhere. It has been trapped in these dark underground waters, so the eyes have been bred right out and replaced by other sensory organs; it seldom bumps into even moving things. Standard preferences.*
Above right: Chilodus punctatus. *4½″. Amazon. The most common of the Headstanders. Omnivorous, even greedy – but a nibbler. Its drab colours go well with camouflage in thickets, twigs, branches. Plenty of oxygen in the flowing waters. 78°–86°F (26°–30°C), pH 6·6, DH 6.*

CHAPTER 2
WATER

As humans begin to worry about pollution on their planet a whole new science of ecology has surged to the fore – and its impact on our understanding of tank water has been enormous. Other than the food you give, the tank water has to supply the fish with everything else it needs, but everything – not merely oxygen to breathe, trace elements for health, biogenic salts and helpful nitrates for the environment. It must also be free from harmful nitrites, toxic gases, etc, and be of reasonable 'composition' regarding pH of the acid/alkaline relationship and of suitable DH or hardness. In earlier books I compared tank water to the supermarket – everything the fish needs has to come from there – fresh and wholesome, and it's your job to maintain this, or your fish will wilt and die.

Oxygen is the main requirement, of course, and the large-as-possible air surface of the tank has already been stressed. A rhythmical intake of water by the mouth aerates the fish blood, and 'washes it clean' as the used water is expelled through the gills, past the mass of delicate gill membranes or filaments which absorb the oxygen and other 'good' elements and let out the toxic. An acceleration in the rate of breathing usually denotes a deficiency of oxygen and an excess of carbon dioxide in the blood.

Should these delicate membranes become paralysed by shock or by sudden transfer from one water to another – something that never, positively never, happens to a wild fish (ever heard of one leaving the river to go into another, suddenly!) then death can occur within the hour as the fish either 'bleeds to

Right: Phenacogrammus
interruptus. *Congo Tetra.*
3". Magnificent dorsal and caudal fins,
supra-terminal mouth, clear sheened.
A fast, far, top swimmer.
Clean, clear, bright waters.
Hearty eater, but fairly peaceful.
Likes aeration. 75°–82°F (24°–28°C).

death' because the temporarily paralysed membranes cannot retain the 'good' elements in the blood which are swept out with the surplus water, or cannot absorb the oxygen. The reverse is when the gills cannot eliminate the carbon dioxide or the overdoses of calcium sulphates and magnesium.

Alternatively, the gills are working normally but you, the owner, have allowed the supermarket to foul or to become so unbalanced that the extra work you now throw on the gills of the fish is more than these can cope with. Fish urine is a case in point. If you have allowed too much of this to accumulate then the extra ammonia acid compounds would be more than the gill membranes could possibly eliminate; death would occur, and it would be little use blaming the dealer or the fish. Marines have highlighted this for us all, and the use of an albuminen skimmer, a device to foam off excess urine utilising the air pump is gradually becoming standard.

Balance Even in the case of freshwater tropicals, suppose you had been too mean to get enough plants, or had been too careless and had allowed them to overgrow and overspread, then either case of imbalance could be tipped fatally by an additional outside factor – an extra hour of strong sunlight, a dirt-saturated filter, an overdose of fish food; smells like tobacco, kitchen, airsprays for killing insects, repelling mosquitoes, polishing the furniture, or even lacquering the ladies' hair-do! All in one single hour! White precipitate grains on the plants, dissolving by day, and reappearing in the morning are a certain danger sign as detailed in the Pelham *Manual for Fish Tank Owners*. Briefly, a superfluity of carbon dioxide develops at night (when the plants give off these oxides) and the 'reserve' salts like calcium bicarbonate are used up instead, precipitating the dangerous white separated grains of residual trace elements; then, during the daylight the plants reverse the process by using up the carbon dioxide and by giving off free oxygen which can then react with the white grains, dissolve them, and restore the reserve bicarbonates. But the balance is altogether too fragile for prudence.

This sort of thing happens on an aggravated scale in marine tanks, if only because there are no growing plants and because salt water contains 20 per cent less oxygen than fresh. If in doubt, part changing the water is still a golden rule, particularly as forgotten fragments of food, dead crustacea like shrimps and other molluscs decompose and foul very very rapidly in salt, and pH or DH indicators do not always warn in time.

Chlorine So, if you are not sure of your water try and change it, gradually. The hazard of chlorine is well known, but this dissipates very quickly if the water is splashed, swirled and agitated; or there are plenty of 'anti-chlorine' tablets and liquids sold everywhere.

Fluoride Fluoride is a dreadful problem. Some governments seem determined to force this down all our throats with some talk of saving milk teeth. Trainers of wild animals in zoos and circuses have long used fluoride to tame the ferocious; added to their drinking water, the nerves are affected and the animals become docile. During the 1939–45 war inmates of concentra-

Top : Prochilodus insignis. *12″. For those who want to try big fish from South America. Centre left :* Alestes longipinnis. *Congo Tetra, the Long Finned Characin. 5″. Prominent red-tinged eye, strong black bar at lower caudal peduncle, silver sheened body. Preferences as for the Phenacogrammus interruptus. Centre right :* Moenkhausia sanctaefilomenae. *Red Eye Tetra.* 2¾″. *Paraguay. Hardy, and a firm favourite. Relatively new. Bottom left :* Gasteropelecus sternicla. *Common Hatchet Fish, the most famous of the many varieties. 3″. Amazon. A surface swimmer and a jumper. Likes clean, bright, free-flowing waters. Unhappy in lower levels, cold or dirt. Prefers the protection of a shoal. 75°–82°F (24°–28°C), pH 6·8–7·0, DH 6–10. Bottom right :* Gymnocorymbus ternetzi. *Black Widow.* 2½″. *Paraguay. A good old favourite, now in many variations like the Veiltail. Hardy, lively. Lovely in shoals. 75°F (24°C) upwards.*

tion camps were similarly quietened; prisons are known to have used the same technique to render people amenable.

Boiling the water does not, repeat not, remove the fluoride; nor does ordinary filtration.

No wonder people buy fresh mountain waters, and aquarists turn despairingly to de-ironizing resins and to other somewhat restricted hopes of 'purifying' their waters. Particularly harmful to marines. In desperation try adding some calcium gluconate, which is the basis of several patented additives used to try and make the water safe.

Rainwater Should you decide to collect rainwater please remember that the first few showers wash down industrial pollutants that would do more harm than good; it is best to wait till the rain has fallen steadily for a while, and has also washed clean the collecting dishes and catchment areas.

pH and DH pH and DH are now familiar terms, with lots of gadgets for reading their scales and for altering them.

pH, or the degree of acidity or alkalinity, in freshwater tropicals effectively goes from 6·0 (extreme acid) to 7·0 (neuter), to 8·0 (extreme alkaline); in the case of marines which are usually kept round the 8·1 to 8·3 mark the alkaline or salt range extends from 7·0 to 14·0 (see page 50). Heavily diluted Hydrochloric acid, or peat, or tree bark will make water acid; bicarbonate of soda or calcium carbonate will do the reverse, both can be introduced via the filter.

As a guide, the tap water of London varies round DH 16–18; the river waters of the upper River Negro where the Cardinal Tetras come from is DH 4–6.

If the pH or DH in your tank fluctuates unduly, then look for some causative factor. It can be excessive evaporation, making you top up say 10 per cent new water per week, which can of itself triple your DH in one month. Is your top light cover ill-fitting? Is the ambient air temperature very different from that of the water in the tank? Why not try insulation, e.g. stick polystyrene or plastic foam onto the tank sides and rear, even base. Is the evaporation really from an over-opened top filter? Would it be a good idea to put a heater in the filter too? Have you checked the water flow as mentioned below?

Filters Increasingly viewed as important is not merely the volume of filter flow, but its direction and penetration. Please remember this when you have sulky fish refusing to eat. With water emerging from the filter pipe, always at the same rate, always in the same direction, you tend to get static eddies and flows with pockets and areas 'unswept' where decomposition runs riot like the festering shallows found round tideless pool edges. Many a careful aquarist will periodically 'wash out' his undergravel filter by forcing water in the reverse direction down the normally-outflowing pipe; many a successful breeder always tops up the tanks, marine included, by always thus filling right from the very very bottom upwards with the new water being introduced from *under* the undergravel filter.

The maximum copper content in water for health is ·01 parts per million; if you are in doubt you can always add *to the filter*

¼ gram of citric acid crystals to a pint of water and then from

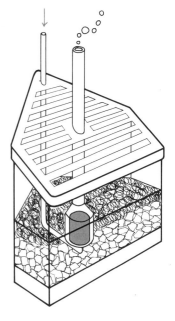

this stock solution put 1 cc per gallon (into the filter) and allow to percolate through to the tank. To repeat, length × width × height in feet × $6\frac{1}{4}$ = number of gallons, less displacement by corals, rocks, etc.

Marines rely heavily on filtration and even more especially on really strong surges and eddies as are constantly found round coral reefs, with splashing masses of released oxygen bubbles – all in dancing sunlight. So the whole art of filtration has been better catered for, to the relief of the tough little freshwater tropicals who had grimly survived man's earlier efforts.

In the old days you just stuck in some activated carbon, some nylon wool, and sat back smirking in self-satisfaction because the fish 'lived', i.e. endured. Came the marines, which died – expensive deaths – and the smirking self-satisfaction gave way to intelligent questioning. How big was the filter area? How quickly did it saturate? What happened when the saturated filter poured poisoned water back into the tank? What was the rate of flow? How far round the tank did it go? What were the areas left to rot and foul?

If you use an undergravel filter because it keeps the top sand clean and nice, what's happening underneath? Is the dirt just swept under the carpet or is there truly a biological change going on producing helpful nitrates?

The more expensive the dead fish, the more truthful the answers. Urine, for example, gives rise to ammonia wastes (NH_3). Normally a fish excretes 3 cu mm of urine per kilogram of body weight per 24 hours, i.e. $\frac{1}{10}$ oz per 2·2 lb of weight. This is changed into urea, a nitrogen excretion, but to effect this change needs 'energy' and in a crowded tank the energy should have been left to do other jobs and 'not be taken from the fish'. Under such crowding (and excess urine) ammonia is excreted

Left: Undergravel filter.
Centre: Nematobrycon palmeri. *Emperor Tetra. 3". Paraguay. Beautiful new favourite; magnificent gleaming eye, and blue sheen over top half of its body. Peaceful and hardy. Likes warm, soft, clean waters.*
Right: Anostomus anostomus. *7". Beauty from South America. Fine by itself, even with small fish or shoals. Two or three tend to squabble; they must have a home of their own. Provide at least four homes for three fish; the extra one makes them all feel unthreatened. Preferences as for the Headstanders.*

31

from the gills, and not from the kidneys as urea is; the more the crowding, the higher the temperature, and, especially, the more alkaline (salt) the water – the greater the harmful ammonia. Above pH 8·4 the harmful ammonia increases even more rapidly, and is one of the main reasons for keeping the pH down to 8·3. The excess ammonia irritates the gills causing extra-rapid breathing and thickening the delicate membranes so that these then extract less oxygen from the water and the whole cycle becomes worse. Excess ammonia is not removed by mechanical filters since it is dissolved in the water, nor does charcoal or aeration remove it; hence a skimmer (gadget for frothing the water) is essential, once the normal balance has been destroyed and the helpful bacteria are insufficient to metabolize the ammonia into useful nitrates. A water change would help, so would less fish, or less dirt. Green algae growth helps too.

Better external filters have more than the conventional three layers so that whole groups of additional aids can also be incorporated, from peat to crushed coral, chemicals, vitalizers and so forth. For similar reasons a layer of filter wool is frequently placed between the undergravel filter and the tank sand.

Filters have their own heating units within, partly to free the tank of these unsightly necessities, partly as auxiliaries. They are also fitted with top lights, now separately housed on the filters – usually restricted to the two top layers (of a several-storied filter) and often aimed to produce green algae. Ozonizers, ultra-violet ray tubes and albuminen skimmers can, of course, also be incorporated or fed into filters.

There are inside filters with perforated bases, sucking up through the sand – a sort of reverse undergravel filter. The dirt is now drawn up and out, and can be seen and easily removed.

There are filter units linked not only in tiers inside and outside the main tank, but also in multi-purpose banks each de-

Above left: Exodon paradoxus. *Throws its full 6″ about. Guyana. Fast strong swimmer. Eats green foods as well as anything else (including fish) that comes its way. Below: Power filter.*

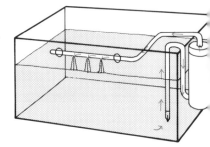

Right: Distichodus sexfasciatus.
10″. West Africa. Beauty. For its size,
relatively peaceful. Vegetarian.
Prefers clean flowing waters but easily
puts up with mulm and debris.

signed for a specific job and all dovetailed into one. The simplest
and most frequently used of these would be a triple unit of an
undergravel filter, plus an external one, plus a heavy-output
airstone – to give real movement of water with appreciable
eddies and surges, truly cleansing. The extra initial cost is soon
repaid in healthy fish and in reduced maintenance, not to mention the restoration of that smirking self-satisfaction!

Air pumps Also now available is a new flood of air pumps able
genuinely to stand up to the work and claiming truthfully (at
last) to silence.

Laterally positioned diaphragms of vastly improved resilience
have made all the difference to the ubiquitous vibrator pumps.
With double and even multiple outlets, some of them are gluttons for work, and are yet amazingly inexpensive. Controls to
throttle down the airflow often are standard, as are replacement
diaphragms. There is hardly a nation that does not manufac-
ture these cheap and functional pumps in assorted colours,
shapes and sizes; transparent plastic casings that give full views
of the interior working parts are typical of the new types, that
run non-stop for months on end without attention. Also becoming popular are special ozone resistant diaphragms for use with
ozonizers, these should not, of course, be housed directly above
the tank so that they suck back in air already charged with
escaping ozone percolating out of the tank.

Piston pumps, silent and strong, continue to hold their own,
but only just, because of two increasingly serious drawbacks.
First, and worst, they have to be rested or they overheat, and
burn out with continuous running. Secondly they deliver air in
bursts, as distinct from a constant flow. Furthermore, they are
expensive.

The bigger power pumps have received a tremendous boost
from technical breakthroughs. The Americans perfected the **33**

Serrasalmo rhombeus.
Piranha. Even bigger than the red,
growing to 14″ in diameter, from
Guyana. Preferences as for S. nattereri.

magnetic coil rotator, and the Germans the water-cooled motor. Both are silent, both are really strong, both will run unattended for months and months; and both have been copied by all nations and are available everywhere in many forms. The Australians and the Americans have modified the European idea and now place the power motor above an external filter, again drawing up right from below and really pouring forth from above; and, like the others, using multi-chambered or multi-layered filters; landscaped side by side, or terraced one above the other.

Very often the return flow of the cleaned water of these power filters is ejected through a rosette like a garden hose spray, or through a tubular-length slotted and holed to taste. Both trap enormous quantities of air bubbles which are injected dancing and foaming into the tank. The joy is that you can control the amount of bubbles from maximum literally to zero, merely by altering the distance the return flow travels before reaching the tank surface; a gap of 2″ or 3″ gives a real curtain of air bubbles shooting *down* towards the bottom, and a lovely sound of falling water. If returned at water surface and directioned diagonally across, some bubbles will constantly sweep clear the surface scum that tends to foul floating foods; but if returned below water surface, the sound, movement and bubbles all vanish.

Modern fish tanks increasingly have the filter chambers actually built into them, particularly the fibreglass, plastic, and models designed for marines or for more expensive freshwater fish. The object is partly to hide unsightly functional gadgets – the heating units can be housed there too – and partly to give really large filter chambers running the entire rear length of the tank and even overlapping the corners. Very neat indeed. Varied systems of holes and slots allow access for air lines, flex and so forth. A short gap of 1″ or so at the bottom of the total length of the base rear is also normal; but the top rear length of the filter wall should be capable of rising up to water level or beyond – of course, this filter wall is inside the tank, parallel to the rear glass and separated off by a couple of inches.

Airstones Sharply upgraded, too, have been the airstones so often used with the pumps, resulting in 'boosted air lifts' which have not merely one tube from the air pump pushing up the air, but a second tube linked to an airstone housed in a bubble-like swelling in the tube of the same air lift, resulting in a truly powerful rush of water.

In the old days, the airstone got clogged quickly, was of one size, shape and colour, and that was that. Now they can be several inches long, 6″–10″ being quite normal, or even stretched the length of the tank. They are pliable too, being of the new plastic compounds and can not only be cut to length but easily hand-bent to shape – a curve, a corner, a square, or whatever.

Wooden diffusers for marines are giving way to new plastic foams like plyamide; even carbon and wool in filters are yielding to them. And, of course, there are many lovely colours to pick from.

Furthermore the simple airstone is being refined or replaced **35** by 'cartridges' that allow a swirling foaming exit after having bathed the water in carbon, filtered off tobacco fumes in an 'air purifier', or added medicines, vitamins, foods, salts, or tonics. Multi-plus chambers are on the market, or are made by the handyman, where you group several cartridges together to form a composite 'cure-all' cartridge cum airstone.

About the only thing that (as yet!) does not have a built-in airstone is the floating breeding trap – though no doubt it'll come. We already have aeration on gadgets for breeding brine shrimps, for keeping tubifex worms, for powering 'vacuum cleaners' for the tank interiors, for moving waterwheels, for floating divers, so why not for the baby fish?

Conversely many aquarists are dropping the airstones altogether in favour of 'funnels'. An ordinary household funnel (plastic, please) as used for pouring liquids into bottles or other narrow-necked containers, is chosen for size, say 5″ wide cup, has a small hole perforated near the joint of the cup to the funnel stem, to house the pipe from the air pump. Excessively simple

Serrasalmo brandti.
Pirambeba. Large. Amazon.
The famous Piranha, ferociously carnivorous, especially when in large shoals. Otherwise rather drab and not specially interesting.
Right: Combined heater/thermostat.

and efficient, you place the wide cup-end downwards into the sand, leaving the stem sticking upwards in the water. This makes a marvellous 'undergravel' filter with enormous suction power, as there is no airstone to 'consume' any of the air power. Some aquarists cut short the upward turned stem to get even more 'pull' or suction. Others leave most of the tank base absolutely bare, having all the sand (or crushed coral for marines) heaped round the cup of the funnel – entirely eliminating the danger of rotting foods and debris lying unseen. Dealers often use this idea in their big stock tanks.

New ideas come every day; the next one might originate from you, the amateur aquarist or from your dealer – either way you have a fabulous choice, and your fish will be so grateful! So many are the developments from these ideas that they had better be left to the next chapter for elaboration.

Heating Meanwhile tropical fish need heating, and seldom thrive if the heartless owner relies merely on the central heating of the house, which rarely tops 72°F (22°C), let alone when lowered by draughts, opened windows, or lower night settings of the thermostat. Tank heaters and thermostats are so cheap – less than the price of a box of chocolates – are so plentiful, and are so widely available that you have no excuse.

Some tanks have special compartments where you can hide these gadgets away; some aquarists put them in the outside filters, or use 'external' types that stick on to the outside of the glass; some arrange the rocks, corals, plants, and so forth – but all can easily camouflage them.

Heaters The good old oldie that has surged forth decade after decade is still to the fore – the pyrex glass tube housing a coil of heating wire wound round a tubular porcelain core; so cheap, so efficient. We like to lay the pyrex tube flat down at base, parallel to the sand, with the flex completely buried under the sand and threaded along to the rear corner of the tank, taken up neatly right in the corner, over the top and down – all hidden; with the heat rising right from below, leaving no unheated layers where the bottom-dwelling fish like the Catfish and eels will freeze and die. Hanging the heater tube down vertically into the tank, stopping short of base level, is deliberately asking for trouble, for 'water stratification' as cold layers are encouraged, and your filter flow may or may not be strong enough to cope with cold spots – the real source of many an 'unexplained' fish mope.

Of course, there are variations on the common heater; very long thin ones to give a greater spread of heat (and a greater chance of breakage); rubber-covered flexible heating coils to be buried under the sand in any chosen pattern – most useful for vivariums for example; great big tough ones, metal ones, mini ones for extra small tanks. Even plastic strips, that stick on the outside of the tank, with heating wires embedded in as in the demisted rear windows of motorcars. And all in many wattages – 25, 40, 60, 75, 100, 125, 150 and 200 watts being common.

Heater and thermostat combined This combination has been popularized by the Americans. Right under the thermostat is not the best place to put the heater, thus the dual unit has **37**

to be relatively large; yet people seem to like the idea, and better filtration helps to distribute the heat all over the tank and make the idea workable.

Table of heater strengths In the climate of Southern England we use the following strength of heaters.

Size in inches	Heater strength in watts	Strength of light bulbs in watts	Number of tropical fish Freshwater	Marine (small)
18 × 12 × 12	75–100	1 × 25	18	3
24 × 12 × 12	125–150	2 × 25	24	5
36 × 12 × 12	2 × 125	3 × 25	36	7
48 × 12 × 12	2 × 150	4 × 25	50	9

Draughty places need more heat, darker situations need more light. The size of the tropicals is for 'normal' ones, i.e. freshwater being 1″–2″ and the marines being 3″–4″.

We find it more helpful to use two heaters in the larger tanks, rather than a single of stronger wattage.

Aeration adds 40 per cent to the above fish capacity; power filters (genuinely so!) double it.

Increased tank height adds nothing to the fish capacity but greatly to the requirements of heat, light and filtration, e.g. 24″ × 12″ × 24″ high would need 200W for heat, 2 bulbs × 40w each for light, and a good tough filter flow. But, it would look very nice!

Thermostats Interior thermostats are often of the pyrex test-tube type, housing a bimetallic strip, i.e. a dual strip of two different metals joined lengthwise parallel together, one having a much greater expansion/contraction rate than the other, causing a slight bending of the joint strip which then makes or breaks the electrical circuit – switching off the heater when the desired temperature is attained. A small adjustment screw is usually housed inside the test-tube, less than a quarter of a turn being more than sufficient to produce temperature variations of 3°–7°F (1°–4°C). Again, cheap and efficient, it has defied all attempts to dislodge it. Just watch to see that the terminal electric points are not pitted or burnt. Often a safety fuse is incorporated – merely joining one of the wires with a blob of soft and easily dissolved solder will serve to break the current in case of a short circuit.

If the top light on the tank is not to be fitted closely and all-over, then an external adjustment screw can be housed above the test-tube sealing bung instead of below, so that alterations of temperature setting can be made without removing the bung. Convenient from that point of view it lags in popularity partly because an all-over lighting cover is usual so that a fully submersible thermostat is preferred; and partly because the knob tends to allow condensation to drip down the central stem, a problem not yet happily solved even by the dust covers fitted by some manufacturers.

Most people who want the ease of rapid temperature adjustments usually buy a thermostat that clips on to the outside of the tank glass, being held in place by a metal clip, a rubber suction

Phenacogrammus interruptus. *Congo Tetra. Relatively new favourite. Unobtrusively beautiful rather than flamboyant. Largish. Likes half lights at oblique angles, and warmth of 80°F (27°C) upwards.*

pad, or by glue. Many are obtainable, and seem popular in spite of their slightly ungainly appearance, and the built-in hazard of well-meaning friends or inquisitive children who twiddle the knob completely to alter the temperature setting. Again the dust caps of the makers only partly solve this. They are particularly useful for very shallow tanks where the extra length of the test-tube type might be awkward unless the mini-length ones are used.

Two useful tips can be noted: (a) if the water is too shallow for your test-tube thermostat, then place it in a glass of water which itself stands in the tank, taking its temperature from there even though its top few inches protrude above water-level; (b) always have the tube standing vertically or any angle will affect the make/break action of the bimetallic strip giving unnecessarily wide fluctuations.

Thermometers Thermometers used just to be of the floating type, made of a spirit column (cheap and unreliable), or of mercury. Now the coil-spring type has added a whole new range with several advantages. It is easier to read the markings, and these don't fade; the unit is smaller and far less obtrusive and can be inside or stuck on to the outside of the tank. The Centigrade scale is rapidly displacing the Fahrenheit scale in common usage. Here is a conversion table:

Centigrade	Fahrenheit
15	59·0
16	60·8
17	62·6
18	64·4
19	66·2
20	68·0
21	69·8
22	71·6
23	73·4
24	75·2
25	77·0
26	78·8
27	80·6
28	82·4
29	84·2
30	86·0
31	87·8
32	90·0
33	91·4
34	93·2
35	95·0

To convert Centigrade to Fahrenheit, multiply by 9/5 and then add 32.

To convert Fahrenheit to Centigrade, subtract 32 then multiply the result by 5/9.

Marines As already stressed several times all metal clips and parts have to be isolated from the water or the spray action of **40** the air pumps. Metal clips can be threaded through plastic

Barbs, Rasboras, Danios and Minnows, etc. (Cyprinidae)

Previous page: Capoeta tetrazona.
Tiger Barb or Sumatra Barb. 3". The
famous Barb that everyone loves:
beautiful football jersey markings on a
reddish body with tipped fins.
Left: the Albino variation.
Terminal mid-water mouth, not
aggressive, but with the hidden barbels
indicating a constant appetite. High
colouring well-defined; asking for strong
light and heavy vegetation to give shaded
patches. Humped shaped back, so not a
far swimmer, but distinctly mobile
judging from its sensible finnage.
The eyes are not bright as in the rest of
the Barbs but have a masking black
stripe – so a preference for clear water
would be reasonable and room to grub in
the shade.
Important is the point of heavy excreta
and urine given off by these restless fish;
so the water can be hard, soft, hot or
even coldish, cluttered or free,
but filtered; really filtered. Otherwise
you'll find them moping head down,
or nosing water surface as though looking
for oxygen – fresh areas. Filtration must,
just must, keep up with excreta,
urine and harmful nitrite bacteria –
whether helped by water changes or not.
Left: Capoeta titteya. *2". Ceylon.*
One of the smallest and most loved,
the upper one being the male.
The intensity of the male breeding colours
is indicative of his passion; the female
may need protective thickets to escape to.
Lovely in a shoal in a small bright clean
tank.
Right: Puntius conchonius.
Rosy Barb. 5". India. An old old oldie.
Survives any conditions, but glows in the
warm rose body coloration.
Normal Barb preferences (see Capoeta
tetrazona).

Previous page: Barbodes everetti.
Clown Barb. 5″. Malaysia.
Bronze/gold sheened body and gleaming
blue/green markings. Peaceful.
Males are smaller, more red finned.

Right: Barbodes schwanenfeldi.
Tinfoil Barb. Up to 15″; one of the
biggest. Silver sheened, re-tinged fins
especially the anal; the dorsal is also
trimmed with black. As is usual with
such deep bodies they require plenty of
clear deep waters. They can jump for
their food, and can eat greens if other
are lacking. Somewhat restless for a
Barb.

Below: Rasbora heteromorpha.
*Harlequin. 1¾″. Malaysia, Thailand,
China, and India. The most famous
Rasbora of all; in many varieties.
Typical of their family. Beautiful
clear-cut markings, warm body colours,
dainty mouth, all proclaiming defence.
Hence like shoals; well camouflaged like
Neon Tetras under overhanging
vegetation (above the water), with clear
bright waters for limited swims.
Its warm, happy colours gives the key
to the high temperatures it prefers.
75°–80° F (24°–27°C), pH 6·0–6·5,
DH 2–4.*

Left: Danio malabaricus. *Giant Danio. 5″. Ceylon. Darkish black, silver sheened body, threaded in between by longitudinal pale blue and gold. Grows rather too large for most tanks – it swims far and very fast – but is peaceful with fish of its own size. Needs clean, clear, brightly lit waters, and likes planted areas for rest.*

Below: Brachydanio albolineatus. *Pearl Danio. 2″. Burma. A good old favourite. Ever moving top-water inhabitant. Lovely in shoals, flashing its blue/green sheen brightly flecked with pearl white.*
With their typical supra-terminal mouths, bodies, and fins built for speed (but not endurance), Danios are ideal in an ever-surging, intertwining, follow-my-leader shoal. They eat anything, including their eggs, and spawn readily. Clean bright waters with overgrowing shade above the water is ideal; a few floating twigs and plants help.

tubing, for instance. Most dealers now have equipment specially adapted for marines, even special bungs in the thermostat tubes to replace the more easily perishable rubber.

Salt water Artificial salts have long solved the problem of getting good salt water for the home tank. Every dealer adds his own pet formula for 'trace elements', and for other additives, and nearly all of them work fine. The real missing unit – the vital, yet unsolved, factor that makes marine fish difficult to keep – is the teeming millions of live plankton found in natural waters. These are always present, although especially abundant in particular seasons like spring and autumn. That's really what the fish miss, and prevents progress. Plenty of artificial plankton, or their substitutes, are marketed, but not with full success. Solve this, and a fortune is yours; it is the biggest single drawback by far in the keeping of marines.

Many are the published formulae for you to make your own sea salt, and hence sea water, but the old favourite is:

Water	96·4 parts
Rock salt	2·8 parts
Magnesium chloride	0·4 parts
Magnesium sulphate	0·2 parts
Calcium sulphate	0·1 parts
Potassium chloride	0·1 parts

The blunt fact is that ocean water varies as much as land water; not merely with locality, but with the seasons and temperature, with storms, earthquakes, and man all lending a hand. Depth of water could also be noted.

Plankton is the constant missing factor; and Mother Nature's huge changes is the other; changes both rhythmic and spasmodic.

As elsewhere stated mix the contents of your salt pack into 10–15 per cent less than the recommended water; if the tap water is already aged the specific gravity readings can be taken in six hours, otherwise in 24; stir well (not with metal!) and aerate heavily, stirring from time to time if the excess salt settles in the bottom of the container (no metal parts!). At last, you can take the specific gravity readings (temperature correct?) adding tap water till the required reading of 1·025 at 75°F (24°C) is reached.

If to be stored, then darkness is preferred to light; before re-using why not filter it through nylon and aerate for a day, before introducing to the aquarium?

If in doubt about your water, separate it off and heat to 140°F (60°C) for 24 hours, allow to cool and keep aerated (also filtered if possible) for three days; if still cloudy, then re-heat again and repeat the process until clear. Never use it unless it *does* clear!

Specific gravity The specific gravity of the water in a tropical marine tank is normally 1·022–1·025 or even 1·028; some advise a rigid control of possible fluctuations, others are far more lenient. Temperature has a bearing on specific gravity, of course, so that the hydrometer used must be calibrated at known **49**

temperatures; the earlier ones were usually set to give true sp. gr. readings at 60°F (16°C). Newer models are set to give correct readings at 75°F (24°C).

Specific gravity expresses the weight of the water; 'salinity' the strength of the salt. Salinity is shown as a percentage of the salt content, say 3·0–3·6 per cent or in parts per thousand, e.g. 30–36.

Hence, two tips: (a) take a glass of the water to be tested and carefully adjust the temperature to the setting before taking the corrected reading which can then be marked on the hydrometer for future readings; (b) please remember that the salts and trace elements take up to 24 hours or more to dissolve, so the water should be aerated at relatively constant temperature all this time first before attempting to take a reading.

Also helpful is a mark on the tank glass at the water-line, so that evaporation is readily noticed. Tap water should be 'aged' before use in topping up – at least the chlorine gases should have evaporated.

pH (degree of acidity or alkalinity) As stated earlier a pH of 8·3 is acceptable, some aquarists preferring pH 8·1 or pH 8·5 and some being far more rigid over this than others. Sodium biphosphate will make the water more acid, sodium bicarbonate will make it more alkaline; all chemicals being dissolved first in water, are introduced gradually (preferably via the filter), and enough time being allowed for thorough circulation before attempting readings. From time to time waters are found to be 'buffered', i.e. resistant to pH changes to an unusual degree. In such cases sodium bicarbonate may be a little slow and clumsy, and need a boost. Your chemist or specialist dealer would help – so too would a cautious dose of washing soda which is basically sodium carbonate. Alternatively a calcium carbonate solution can be used. Many enthusiasts make it by crushing (cleaned) shells which they introduce to make the water alkaline, or, if in a hurry, they mix these shells crushed to a powder in a cupful of hot water till most dissolve, and pour in that – the surplus calcium carbonate settling as a white precipitate powder.

It is important, very important, to make all changes of water, of pH, of DH, of temperature, or filtration, gradually. Fish are then far more likely to benefit. Marine enthusiasts nearly always seem to find it prudent to keep stored (dark and cool) reserve salt water ready mixed and aged; after all, they can't just turn on the tap to get more. Nor do they tend to throw away the used water, preferring to let it settle, to siphon off carefully, to correct its specific gravity or pH, and then to keep – if only to wash sea sand or coral in or to add as a seasoner to a newly made-up batch of salt water. Enthusiasts who do this often also concern themselves with the salinity (as distinct from the specific gravity as already discussed) of their water, i.e. of the parts per thousand of salt in it. Normal salinity could well be represented by 34·0 parts per thousand, giving a specific gravity of 1·025 at 60°F (16°C).

Further tips Partial changes of marine water are particularly helpful say every month, three months and six months, in

increasing proportions of 15% to 30% to 50% if only because

Right: Puntius nigrofasciatus. *Ruby Barb. 2½". Ceylon. 'The poor man's Tiger Barb' is an undeserved jibe – in breeding colours the diffused red of the male body is most attractive. Very resilient to indifferent water conditions.*
Below right: Capoeta tetrazona. *Tiger Barb. 3". A relative newcomer. Slightly less boisterous, with lovely breeding hues tinging its albino flanks.*
Below: Hydrometer.

man's knowledge is not yet sufficient to dispense with this rough-and-ready aid. Many are the stories told, however, of 'never having changed my water in two years'; true enough – to a point, but water change still helps, or at least a water 'turn round'– to take some and to store it in a glass container in the dark, and replacing it with that which had been stored. Darkness seems particularly beneficial; sunlight, on the other hand, seems to activate the undesirable so much that it swamps the desirable.

Another very useful rough-and-ready precaution is to soak everything beforehand that will come into contact with the salt water – the filter, its carbon (especially), its wool, the inside of the tank (including corners), corals, rocks, sand, etc – everything. An ultra-strong saline solution, some three times the normal intensity, is usual; and then a rinse out in 'aged' freshwater or in normal salt water. Similarly too, the gravel or crushed coral of the tank should be washed in *salt* water, not in fresh, so as not to destroy the helpful nitrates and other positive microscopic life that is present. New sand, etc needs a wash in tap water only and then a soaking in salt water, as already suggested. Often this new sand/coral can be 'seeded' by the addition of some that has already matured in the tank.

Mixing the artificial salts into the water poses a problem. Suppose your packet of artificial salts is enough for 50 litres, and you want only to use 10, you might be tempted to take a fifth of the salt and dissolve that in 10 litres, but that could bring trouble; the trace elements and other compounds are not necessarily evenly distributed in the solid salts, and the one-fifth you took out would almost certainly not have a uniform proportion of the total elements. Hence it means mixing the whole 50 litres,

Above: Puntius ticto.
$3\frac{1}{2}''$. *Ceylon. Similar to the* P. stoliczkanus, *except that the tail spot is its main feature. Hardy and peaceful favourite. Likes a clean home.*
Left: Rasbora elegans.
$5''$. *Malaysia. Note the firm mouth, capable body and trim fins. Can easily look after itself. Tends to mind its own business and stay at home.*

using 10, and storing the remaining 40. A nuisance!

If you simply cannot bear to make up the whole 50 litres, and then have the problem of storing the remaining 40 litres, there is a compromise: mix up all the salt into a small amount of water (measured and remembered), and then use a few drops of this ultra-strong salt solution to bring your aged tap water up to the desired specific gravity. The unused stock solution would be easier to store than the 40 litres.

Incidentally, if you are mixing the whole 50 litres it would be better to add slightly less than the recommended amount first, then to stir and to aerate for 24–48 hours, and finally to add the remaining water a little at a time, checking the specific gravity readings as you go.

Cooling the water can be a bigger problem than heating. Ice cubes in a plastic bag, sealed by twisting the neck and securing with a rubber band, can be dropped in; later to be removed. A coil of plastic tubing can be immersed in the tank and then have cold water from the tap surge through – of course the end of the coil is outside the tank and running to waste.

The human sense of smell is often used by experienced aquarists the water and contents must smell right. A very useful tip, this. If in doubt, part change, or increase the rate/direction of the filter flow.

If you have used copper sulphate or other chemicals to kill harmful bacteria, the new generation of the surviving bacteria may well have become resistant to this chemical; you might need a new one for the second dosage. The same applies, unfortunately, to ozonizers and to ultra-violet light rays; those that survive the initial dose tend to become resistant to the following ones.

Right: Puntius schuberti.
Golden Barb. 3½". Orange fins and
striking black marks. Peaceful and
much loved. Lovely in shoals.
Below right: Puntius stoliczkanus.
2½". Burma. Relatively new. Fine red
dorsal flecked with black; bronze
sheened body featuring peduncle spot and
red flecked eye.

CHAPTER 3
EQUIPMENT

The choice before the aquarist can truly be described as fabulous; even the fastidious can have little difficulty finding what he wants.

Heaters and thermostats, filters and pumps, lights, tanks, and stands, have already been discussed. There remains a kaleidoscopic mass of supplementary aids from the frivolous to the very serious ozonizers, the ultra-violet ray tubes, and the urine skimmers. These three aids are relatively new and have been forced by marine experiments, are improving rapidly, and will surely end by being standard equipment long before the 1980s.

Ozonizer The ozonizer blows into the tank intensely activated O_3 (oxygen) instead of the normal O_2 particles, and can exterminate bacteria like a space gun – unfortunately, all bacteria including the healthful and the positive. Unfortunately, too, stronger doses would not only kill the bacteria, but the fish as well. As our understanding of the problem grows, and as we learn to use this great power, the popularity of the ozonizer is bound to increase. Diffusion of the O_3 by introducing it into the filter first, or by bouncing it off a protective shield or rock, or by using a mixture chamber, or by steering the activated flow in chosen directions – for example away from the lowest strata of the undergravel filter if the biological balance is beneficial there – are all obvious safeguards. So also is the idea of short bursts of this O_3, say an hour after feeding time when uneaten food has been left around, or shortly after the introduction of new fish; both can be alternated with persistent very low strength doses lasting two or three days – or even being continuous, at mild doses of 2–3 mgs/ozone/power per 10 gallons.

As yet the arguments rage and no-one need be afraid of making individual experiments. Many strengths of ozonizers are marketed, and nearly all have a sliding adjustment control scale, so you can have considerable scope: sterilizing an empty tank from which diseased fish have been temporarily or recently removed can now be done in seconds or at least in minutes, without having the bother of dismantling, boiling, disinfecting, etc, etc. Green algae can be killed at a stroke, and the resulting sediment just siphoned off, obviously with the filter switched off. Foods like tubifex worms are easily treated before feeding to the fish.

What the ozonizer will not do is to get at virus inside the fish, or under their mucus coating, at least not directly; but the range

of the O_3 is the entire tank unit including the filters, and for

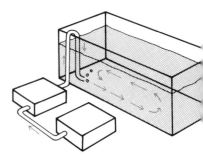

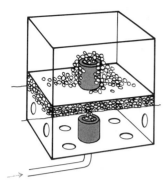

instance, once the protective cyst of white spot breaks, the O_3 would prevent infection of other fish by the free-swimming spores. Also the O_3 in the water is compulsorily swallowed by the fish and can damage the delicate gill membranes if too strong, hence the preference of some aquarists for the ultra-violet ray tube.

Ultra-violet ray tube The ultra-violet ray tube's range is strictly limited to its immediate vicinity. It is often housed separately, the water flowing past its influence, being fed back to the filters and then on to the tank. A radiation of 3 watts with a throughput rate of 600 gallons per hour can be used for days on end. This means that invertebrates like anemones can be kept in a marine tank with fish – which would not have been possible if copper sulphates were being used to clear the tank of hostile bacteria, the anemones being vulnerable to such chemicals. Its power and its drawbacks are otherwise similar to those . of the ozonizer.

Urine skimmer The urine skimmer is another vital new gadget made possible by the introduction of stronger air pumps. Its operation is simple in the extreme – blow enough air into a restricted chamber into which the tank water is being forced to cause froth and foam; these slimy bubbles are then trapped in an upper-storey of the chamber, or even a separate upper chamber, where they soon burst and subside into a nasty yellowish liquid, fish urine.

Increasingly popular is the practice of combining this 'reactor tube' with an ozonizer or ultra-violet ray light played into the foaming mass of bubbles prior to their settlement as the yellowish liquid.

Nitrite checks Rapidly demanding a place for itself is the gadget to check the 'nitrate level' of the water, i.e. the balance between the helpful nitrates and the hostile nitrite bacteria. This is symptomatic of many refinements as the aquatic hobby grows and has more resources lavished on it. Not impossible is the day when all imports and newly-caught specimens will be put through sterilization chambers on a really big scale before dispatch to the retailers. In fact the experiment started at large fish farms in California at the beginning of the 1970s.

Gadgets Matching that huge scale dealer-breeder development is a fascinating flood of gadgets for the home aquarist. These include:

aerated holders to keep fresh tubifex worms; to breed brine shrimp eggs;

tongs and tweezers with long handles to function under water;

power-operated vacuum cleaners, motivated by air pump, torch battery, or even by hand bellows, all with or without disposable refuse bags;

ornaments that aerate as well, like divers, moving water-wheels, hovering 'space ships' that zoom and fall to rise again; shells that open and close releasing large bubbles or streaming small ones, and 'volcanoes' that erupt;

automatic electric fish feeders, a sort of time clock, dropping pre-set foods at pre-set times; the latest models can work several months on end!

Above: Urine Skimmer.
Below left: Ozonizer.
Below: Holder for tubifex worms.

breeding traps that float, or clip, to hold the eggs or the fry; or, a cruel version, to release the fry into the main tank below as food for difficult fish like Cichlids or marines;

fish catching nets with ultra close mesh to trap even small daphnia, or of a fast-flowing nylon for rapid movements below water level if you're trying to catch a Khuli eel whose acceleration and swerves would put a racing car to shame;

nylon done up as spawning grass to protect small fish; adaptable to shape, colour, texture, and density;

artificial plants of every colour and shape, for stringing in places where natural plants could not possibly grow, for hiding the heaters and filter tubes;

artificial rocks, often made of plastic, singly, in groups, as walls, or as complete aquascapes;

special scrapers for plastic tanks, for hard green algae (not merely razor blade holders but a sophisticated netting or foam compound);

vitamins, foods, plant killers, plant fertilizers, tonics, medicines; you just name it – your dealer will get it!

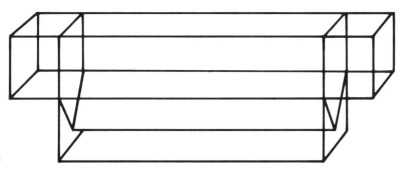

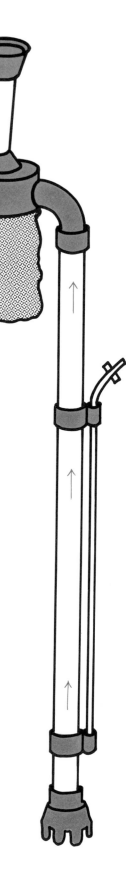

CHAPTER 4
PLANTS

Not only for their beauty but for their function are plants essential for the balanced tank; it is merely a tragedy that they cannot yet be easily used with marine fish.

Planting medium If the emphasis were solely on the plants themselves then all manner of special soils and fertilizers could be used. In the home fish tank, where the balance of all factors is more important than the plants, aquarium sand proves adequate for growth and for the maintenance of photosynthesis, i.e. the cycle whereby harmful carbon dioxide gases given off by the fish is broken down by the plants into oxygen and carbon, the oxygen going back to the fish, and the carbon compounds acting as fertilizers for the plants.

Points to watch The right balance between top light, sand, plants, fish, fish droppings, and foods, is very easy to attain – almost automatic in fact. An excess of light (natural, artificial or a combination of both) produces green algae. A sand depth of 1″–2″ is enough for a tank up to 18″ tall. A plant selection that covers, in clumps, lines or clusters, about a third of the floor surface should normally serve a fully-stocked tank. Not too sparse, not too overgrown; not too tall and trailing all over the water surface, but pruned back to below water-level, leaving just the small proportion to trail and float. If you mix the light and the dark greens, the tough big shade-giving leaf with the delicate, the fern with the grass and the reed, you can't go wrong.

If it looks right, then it probably is right.

Tell-tale danger signs are the white precipitate grains; dark patches in the sand immediately round the roots denoting too many harmful nitrites as distinct from beneficial nitrates, and a clean up is *urgently* wanted. A plant that sulks, changes colour, has stunted or deformed foliage is asking for a change of temperature or light, more room for its roots, or less heat *below* its roots. Pruning could help, so could a fertilizer pellet inserted at its base, or a liquid for its leaves. The bigger the leaf the more the plant tends to get sustenance from the foliage rather than solely from the roots. Mulm at the base or smothering the leaves is obvious; not so is incorrect pH or DH, but both are important. Planting too deep, i.e. below the crown, is asking for trouble.

If in doubt part change the water, or alter the temperature by 2°F (1°C) depending on the season – in spring you raise, in autumn you lower. Similarly with the duration or intensity of the top lighting – in spring more, in autumn less as the plants tend to 'rest'.

Hints The lighter green the leaf, the more the plant tends to oxygenate. The bigger the plant the more difficult it is to transplant and the more likely to shed its leaves. So please don't be too greedy when buying 'that big one'!

Tall plants get stalky as the bottom leaves drop off; nearly always this happens with those that propagate from cuttings, rather than from runners sprouting below sand level from the parent crown. The cure is simple – nip off the lowest and stalkiest part, and replant the top bit that still has foliage; it will soon take root.

If the fish drive you mad because they keep uprooting everything, first make sure that they are not simply asking for more varied foods – eating the same unchanged stuff day after day, no wonder they chew the plants in desperation – then you can plant the cuttings not directly into the gravel, but first into porous and holed containers which are then embedded in. The holes in the containers should be big enough for the roots to spread out later. Decorative or plain flowerpots can be used, of course, but so can all manner of originalities – a clear, almost transparent 4″ plastic tube cut to a short length just to protect the vital areas, leaving the roots and the top both free, is an example to start you on your own search. Ever tried using the gently fluorescent coloured plastics that shed a softly flowing glow on to the plant and then reflect back to you?

Plastic plants Artificial plastic plants have a place too. The old-fashioned sniff-sniffs recoil in horror from the idea, but others don't. Lovely colours, beautifully made; most useful in speciality situations and circumstances; easily blended and mixed with the growing ones – a fantastically wide choice. If used for marines the good old rule of pre-soaking in extra strong solution of salt is sensible; some plastics react to this treatment or even disintegrate. All plants should be free of metal wires or clips, and their glues should be non-toxic; there is little reason why you could not re-make your own sprays using the new aquarium rubberized sealers; it would be safe, and it could be original – would it shock you too much to incorporate pieces of wood, rock, coral, and such like?

Indigenous conditions The joy of the aquatic trade is that it caters for all types – there are people who fall hook, line and sinker for the plants, and feature these above other aspects like fish, which are kept merely as fertilizers because of their droppings; with tank heights and tank lightings all subserving the plants. For such enthusiasts the following additional data might help.

When transplanting dig out the plant, don't pull it out; take the surrounding soil too, if this is not possible then don't 'tear up', but having dug up, wash out the roots, all of them, ready to reposition as firmly based as possible later. A fertilizer tablet, or a lump of clay-like soil, the size of the tip of your little finger, placed directly under the plant always helps, if you feel this to be necessary.

The lighter green the plant, the more fast growing it is, the more food it needs, the more it sheds its leaves which tend to be small or thin and the more it needs a 'rest' in winter. While

Above left: Spatterdock.
Above right: Echinodorus intermedius.
Below left: Cryptocoryne willisii.
Below right: Hygrophila guianensis.

thriving in summer the more it keeps down green algae partly by competing directly for the same 'food' and partly because the algae cannot get a real grip on its relatively quick-changing foliage.

The slower-growing types can be left unpruned and unattended for a couple of years if you like – but watch out lest they slowly alter the water pH to suit themselves, to the detriment of the fish whose health then definitely plays second fiddle to plant growth. Often their leaves have a slightly bitter taste, or at any rate an unappetizing one, and fish seldom nibble into them, although often on them, to get off algae and other microscopic growths attracted by the firm texture of the leaf.

In the tropics, many plants spend the dry hot summer exposed above the water, when they often flower and send up relatively big foliage. In the rainy seasons they tend to get flooded and to be totally submersed – the leaves then shrink, drop and lighten in colour; runners, plantlets and long thread-like shoots multiply. Under rapid transplanting both conditions are manifested – it's only a day or so from hot-moist Singapore to wherever your tank is!

The varieties available literally are ever changing, but the twenty-four that are illustrated are widely available, are well known, and are typical of the range in foliage, size, shape, colouring and propagation. All can be mixed and used in the home aquarium and all are either hot-house grown or imported from warm climates. The cheap, coarse, summer-only growths that you can clump out from the local ditch have not been included; they would normally die in your tank and foul it. For completeness, though, some of the beautiful lilies suitable for outdoor and indoor ponds have been shown, and are worth their place.

Above left: Hygrophila polysperma.
Above right: Elodea ernestiae.
Below left: Elodea densa.
Below right: Aponogeton fenestralis.

The plants

Nuphar sagittifolium Spatterdock or Cape Fear. The most famous of the many nuphars, some of which are sold as seedlings, some with bulbs, or as this is with a knobbly clumpy rhizome. Fast growing, easy to plant, its rhizome appreciates a tiny pellet of soil directly underneath to allow it to re-establish after having been cut from its parent.

Its beautiful, flowing, swaying leaves are much loved by humans, undulating magnificently in aeration like airborne balloons straining at the moorings – and by fish seeking shelter or shade. Their delicate aura is enticing; yet the plant is resilient and will readily expand to 6 cubic inches or more unless pruned. Resistant to algae; it seldom sulks too much, yet its leaves can get pitted if it is cross and wants better conditions.

Echinodorus intermedius This family of bog plants from South America has rapidly established its popularity, and now is widely cultivated. It can grow anywhere, with or without light, in any conditions. Most useful as a centrepiece, or where broad leaves are wanted. Propagates from runners; given food, light, and soil it will surge – denied these it will steadily hold its own, and hence its especial use in dismal corners or where restricted growth is preferred. Don't be surprised if it nags you by changing colour, usually darker; change the water, checking **61** the pH, if you can't bear the nagging any longer.

Cryptocorine willisii Widespread, tough, Malaysian group growing in or out of the water, anywhere and almost anyhow. Would it adapt to marines? It can to brackish. Rapidly changes not merely size of leaves with better/worse conditions but also shape and even colour.

Our specimen is normally found with the crinkled leaf, tending to elongation and to curling, which accentuates under harsh treatment even to dropping off. Lanceolate, from light green to warm brick-brown, with a purple tinge underside. Often 6 cubic inches, or more; 12 are not unknown, nor are a mere 3, if kept down by hard conditions. Typical bitter-tasting leaves, unappetizing to fish. Pitting is a protest, and a plea for a little help. Even if all the leaves drop off, the plant may yet re-emerge in time.

Hygrophilia guianensis Relatively lesser known, darker and tougher; pointed lanceolate leaves some $5'' \times \frac{1}{2}''$, with no particular undershading.

Hygrophilia polysperma Light green, more delicate leaves seldom exceeding 2″ but profuse on a thick woody central stem. Grows tall, anywhere, anyhow. Protests by shedding its lower leaves to flaunt its bare stem at you – can be nipped, the top replanted, or be better treated when it will wave in happy clumps and thickets.

Elodea ernstiae Found everywhere, good oxygenating leaves, in whorls, usually light green, sometimes under tinged with reddish hue. Can get stalky, can break, but replants easily. Stands most temperatures and conditions. Gradually getting better known than its darker, tougher cousin, *E. densa*. Will even survive for an astonishingly long time if merely left floating, when it throws out white distress signals of thin floating, probing runners; recovers at once on replanting.

Elodea densa Like its cousin *E. ernstiae*, this is found but everywhere and grows regardless of anyone or anything. When sulky it is extra brittle, and if that doesn't succeed it becomes slimy. White, thin, probing runners are a sure sign it's hungry.

Aponogeton fenestralis Madagascar lace plant. The most famous of them all. Everyone knows it, wants it, but can't have it – it just does not thrive. So, everyone gives you a pet formula for growth – yet the truth is excessively simple; whoever heard of a cold draught of air in Madagascar (when the plant is luxuriating)? That's your biggest problem – when you lift the tank top light, or even open the door or window.

The finely veined, lace woven, tapering leaves gracefully float gossamer-like in the glory of their 12″–15″ lengths, in the magnificence of their 24″ cube pattern. Loving light and warmth, hating algae and dirt; strong flowing, clean, well-aerated waters (no fish urine please), rich soil, pH 6·8, DH 4–6, and water depth of 18″–24″ at 78°F (26°C) bring forth a superb response. Known to have stopped spoilt and jaded millionaires in their tracks.

One cold draught *including* the one it got *before* reaching your tank, and it demands long careful attentive penance before sitting up to smile. When sulky it produces more stem than leaf.

Above left : Aponogeton crispus.
Above right : Ceratopteris thalictroides.
Below left : Pistia stratiotes.
Below right : Bacopa monniera.

Aponogeton crispus Widely found in Australia, and elsewhere. Typical of the attractive serrated edged leaves, some of which can grow to unbelievable lengths of 20″. Tough and adaptable, it does not need too much light, which makes it particularly useful. As is usual with this shaped lanceolate leaf the slight bitter taste makes it practically hungry-fish proof. When sulking it stays small, or produces more spike than leaf.

Ceratopteris thalictroides Indian Fern. Lovely, tough, grow anywhere, anyhow, favourite. Will even float, unplanted, for weeks and survive. Any bit that breaks off, and this often happens, will replant and grow.

Pistia stratiotes Water Lettuce. Typical of the floating plants that send down grouped roots for nourishment, to the delight and shelter of baby fish. Everyone loves it, except when the tank top tends to scum (too near a kitchen or bathroom smell?) and this rapidly growing plant gets in the way of the daily surface skimming then required.

Bacopa monniera Baby's Tears. An old old favourite, still growing strong round its central pliable stem and its compact oval leaves, profuse in their green scatter. Seldom grows stalky, easy to break, and to replant. Takes kindly to light, warmth and to clustering. A slightly bitter taste inhibits fish from eating it.

Ditto – in flower Allow it to develop tall and strong, and to emerge if it wants; and the flowers come in season.

Bacopa caroliniana This is more stringy and delicately leafed than its cousin *B. monniera*; is tougher, stands almost any temperature and can live submersed or even exposed when it tends to thicken up. Likes light. Grows tall, but can be nipped and transplanted.

Cabomba caroliniaria Again an old old favourite, found wild in the southern states of the U.S.A., right through the jungles and swamps of South America. Many varieties exist of course, like the more spherical *C. aquatica*, but all have the extraordinary delicacy of leaf, in lush finely-feathered whorls, loved by fish and by humans.

When sulking it tends to go slimy, and to disintegrate if abused – over-subjected to dirt and mulm, for instance. Otherwise it stands most waters and temperatures.

Red tinges are encouraged by strong, sustained, lights; algae having been kept down by filters.

Nomaphila stricta Rather like the *Hygrophila* already described though not in fact so related. It is tough, grows tall, right out of water, and groups readily into dense thickets. Vivid green. When sulking covers its leaves with a fine hairline growth.

Myriophyllum brasiliense Another tremendous favourite, second only to the *Cabomba*, and also found in many varieties, everywhere, and in nearly all conditions. Its leaves too are finely feathered in lush profusion causing the pliable stem pleasingly to sway. The whorls are not markedly spherical, but the green is beautiful, full and rich – although not dark or dense. It too has a red tinge developed under strong light.

Slimy when sulking, if you've ignored the earlier danger signal of stalkiness.

Tasty, like the *Cabomba*, the fish love to peck it, as well as on
64 it, even in between its lacing thready leaves.

Fancy Goldfish and Coldwater Fish

Above: Orandas. 6". Originally
China, now home-bred. Typical of the
relatively few beautiful fish suitable for
a coldwater aquarium, this illustration
features the finnage and colour.
The 'lion's mane', or highly-prized
growth of pimply-collar round the head,
is just beginning on these young adults,
slightly larger and older than those
normally available; it grows prominent
from the third year on.

*Previous page : Fantail Shubunkin.
The heavy tail finnage makes it more
suitable for the tank ; the body markings
show through the transparent scales in a
most pleasing way. Blue sheens are
usually the most prized. Peaceful and
hardy.*

*Below : Comet-tailed Shubunkin.
More streamlined, faster swimming,
need more room. Hardy, they can winter
out doors, yet stand quite high summer
temperatures.
'Flock-bred', i.e. groups spawn at a
time, fertilizing the eggs as they are
scattered ; the fish then hunt/eat the
semi-adhesive eggs and fry. Typical of
all the coldwater fish here described.*

*Right : Koy Carp. 20″. Relative
newcomer from Japan, and obviously
here to stay. Many varieties, mostly too
large for tanks and better in ponds.
Very tame, long-lived (40 or more
years), a little lazy/sluggish ;
bright coloured, they are magnificent
in a shoal. Hardy.*

Labyrinths

Betta splendens. *Siamese Fighter.*
Of many many colours – red, blue, green,
and albino predominating – mixed or
pure; with gorgeous finnage, coloured,
translucent, or even transparent;
the strains ever improve. Two males fight
on sight to defend their territory until
one flees, or is killed. Recent attempts
are now directed to improving beauty
rather than pugnacity, e.g. the lovely
clear-tailed ones from Bangkok.
The gorgeous colouring, flaring gill
plates, business-like mouth, and strong
supple 3″ body are obviously for show,
not for camouflage, and attack is clearly
indicated. Not for it the need of
protective thickets but the clear waters as
demanded by its featured eye, and well-lit
as asked by its strong colours.
Algae appreciated. 77°–84°F
(25°–29°C), pH 6·8–7·0, DH 4–6.

Left: Colisa lalia. *Dwarf Gourami.*
2". India. A beautiful favourite;
its preferences have been described in
detail at the beginning of chapter 7.

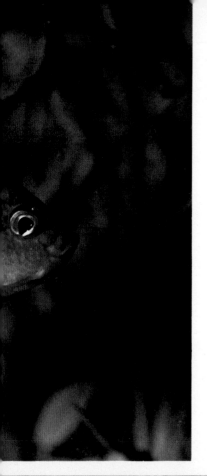

Left: Macropodus concolor. $3\frac{1}{2}''$. *Malaysia. Typical of the many varieties. Not too peaceful, except with larger fish.*

Below: Colisa labiosa. *Thick-lipped Gourami. $3\frac{1}{2}''$. N.E. India. Peaceful.*

Above: Helostoma temmincki.
Kissing Gourami. 10″. Indonesia.
Great favourite. Goes around kissing
anything and anybody. In albino,
in yellow/green, and other shades.
Peaceful.

Right: Polycentropsis abreviata.
African Leaf fish. 4″. River Niger.
A great big open-wide-on-hinge mouth
that eats most fish of its own size, in one
quick lunge. Likes warmth 83°–87° F
(29°–31°C).

Synnema triflorum Water Wistaria. Similar to the Indian Fern with which it is often confused; with the same lovable characteristics. Will grow readily right out of the water, even more eagerly.

Limnophila sessiliflora Ambulia. 'Poor man's *Cabomba*', used to be the name of this graceful plant, half way between that and *Myriophyllum*, both as regards colour and also the fineness and profusion of its leaves; whorl shaped rising up the stem in close following rhythm, opened like lacy umbrellas, of maximum diameter about half way and then tapering to the top. Or, if a more technical description is preferred, the leaf rosettes stand in verticils around the stem.

Stalky when disgruntled, slimy when sulking – in temperatures over 80°F (27°C) for instance. Likes light, but not algae. Tasty – the fish love it.

Ludwigia natans The good old oldie. Tough, developing the lovely red tinges underneath the leaves, especially in the autumn, although this has now been artificially fixed most of the year. The older the plant the more the vivid green darkens in the alternating and opposite leaves. Easily grows out of water. Indigenous to the U.S.A., especially the southern states.

Ludwigia arcuata A relative newcomer, compared to the famous *L. natans*, it is more delicately pointed, and lighter in colour, the small leaves rarely exceeding an inch in length, but being thickly dotted up the stem. Gives a very pleasant, slightly-tangled clump, ideal for fry.

Anubias barteri Unusual arrow-shaped leaves, large, that emerge from the water at the slightest chance. Stand any conditions, especially if they can reach out of water for part of their growth. Biggish growth below sand-level, requires 3″ or more depth for comfort. Not eaten by fish, as you would guess from the strong, dark leaves.

Cryptocoryne griffithii A bog plant like the others of its kind, the *Anubias*, and so many cousins now adapted to the tank. Fish-proof, it can grow fairly large right out of the water; also, it can be held down by cold, cramped, or darkened conditions – surviving tenaciously. In common with heavily-rooted plants it objects to transplanting, and sheds its leaves in disgust. Dark green, the underneath being red shading to purple. Changes colour in protest, and becomes pitted, but is very resilient for all that.

Pontederia cordata Typical of the many other bog plants constantly being introduced. The illustration (on page 76) features the bloom. Most will flower if allowed to grow tall enough and, important this, kept warm and moist as the air in Asian swamps or bogs. Tall tanks featuring fish below and protruding, creeping, jungle-steamy colourful lushness above, the whole being enclosed by the top light that keeps the hot moist air from escaping – all that can have a profusion of such blooms and look striking.

Water lilies Not entirely out of place here is the following selection of water lilies such as may well grace your pond in summer. More and more people are keeping a pond *indoors*, right in the sitting room. The plastic injection moulded ponds started the **73**

Above: Bacopa caroliniana.

Below: Nomaphila stricta.

Above: Cabomba caroliniana.

Below: Myriophyllum brasiliense.

Above: Synnema triflorum.

Below: Ludwigia natans.

Above: Limnophila sessiliflora.

Below: Ludwigia arcuata.

Opposite page.
Above left : Anubias barteri.
Above right : Cryptocoryne
griffithii.
Below left : Pontederia cordata.
*Below right : Collecting aquarium
plants.*

idea which began in England and has spread rapidly to Australia and America.

As mentioned in chapter 1 the pond can easily be brought up to eye level – sinking a hole in the floor is totally unnecessary – on a stand. You can even just plonk it on the carpet – literally.

Add the sound of falling water from a cascading waterfall, some lights (coloured?) submerged or shining down, a nice decorative surround of wood, grass, flowers in pots, etc, etc, etc, and you'll be wondering why you never thought of it before.

Inside, right in the living room, on the landing, in the hall, to fill that alcove, as a room divider, in the waiting room, the outer office, in the presidential suite, the restaurant – it's lovely anywhere.

And just look at these four blooms which are illustrated below: *Marliancea chromatella* (single); *Rene jerard*; *Zantedeschia aethiopica*, Arum lily; *Aponogeton distachyum*, Water Hawthorn.

The typical aquarium bog plant of the *Cryptocoryne*, *Anubias*, *Aponogeton* types which are a little too large for a tank. Look how it would flourish in the indoor pond, growing below and above the water-line *simultaneously*, with different shaped and coloured foliage below water from that which is above.

This page.
Above left : Marliancea chromatella.
Above right : Rene jerard.
Below left : Zantedeschia aethiopica.
Below right : Aponogeton
distachyum.

CHAPTER 5
LAYING OUT
THE AQUARIUM

For the freshwater fish your choice is vast. Chapter 1 has already established the initial basis before the layout can be begun – how big is your tank? How much air surface? How far away from it will you normally view? How high off the ground will your eyes be when viewing?

As was said then, the further away you are the broader the sweep of the internal décor, the more diffused the top lighting, and the more the surrounding room and tank's exterior-cum-top-light come into focus. Close to gives a chance for finesse to be appreciated inside, right inside.

Sand Sand is adequate for the normal balanced tank, unless special emphasis is to be placed on the plants (when some add loam – to the disgust of the fish and of the appearance), or on breeding/rearing when anything goes from intense sterilization to a real old messy nursery.

Above: Orandas. *Firm cold water favourite, originally from China. The large lion-mane growth on the head starts late. Not below 64°F (18°C) for preference.*
Right: A pool arrangement, as set up for an exhibition, showing how to utilize that spare corner.

If the sand is too fine it mats down to choke the plants; if too coarse it traps fallen and hence decaying food particles, more-over the fish love to pick up the sand, to swill it around and to spit it out. In breeding, of course, many many types use sand deliberately to spray on to chosen sites to clean them for the eggs. It's a very deep-rooted instinct.

So the sand has, but has, to be right, just right; otherwise you are building yourself trouble and mopy fish. Here in the heart of London's West End we drag ours all the way from the Channel Islands which means the bother and expense of a sea crossing – as distinct from merely loading a lorry. We also get our coral sand for marines from the Pacific. The official English grading for the particles of this sea sand is one sixteenth of an inch, i.e. holes of that size in a sieve will release such grains. Many people recommend a coarser grain like one eighth, but please please remember that fish must be able to swill it around in their mouths. What suits your undergravel filter is far less important than a centuries old instinct implanted by Mother Nature.

Rocks Rocks, to hold the sand in place and to make a beautiful décor, need care in selection although the choice is wide. Incidentally, where do those moaners come from who object to a pleasing layout because it 'detracts' from the fish? Would you want your wife or daughter to live in a dull cell so as not to 'detract' from her beauty!

If the rock breaks up easily under a hammer or too quickly becomes holed and weathered, then it is almost certainly not

safe; it would dissolve unduly in water, wrecking the pH and

DH. That's just the temptation you must resist. Scrape the rock hard with a knife, hard; if you make no impression then it's likely to be safe. Drop some acid (hydrochloric, for instance) and see if it reacts or ferments; it should remain inert and unpitted. If your tank is to hold marines then it is important to see that metal veins or traces are entirely absent. For the tougher freshwater tank this is less relevant, and even quartz-veined rocks can usually be accommodated – they do dissolve, but slowly, and their beauty is worth the consequent periodic change of water, although not for marines when the safety margins are far too slender. Black Devon rock with its inherent white veins is worth getting hold of; sandstone is not recommended.

Freshwater aquascapes You can soon tell the worth of a really good specialist dealer, who genuinely knows his stuff, as distinct from 'the pet shop man', when it comes to layout. Not for this artist a half circle of plants and three rocks dumped in front which some folks have been brainwashed into believing is a tropical fish tank.

Let us take a tank 36″ long × 12″ wide × 15″ high. In it we would put nearly three-quarters of a hundredweight of washed sea sand (see chapter 6), sloping from 1″ deep in front to some 6″ at the rear; to this we would add another three-quarters of a hundredweight of carefully broken up and hand-picked rocks. The result would be positively beautiful when some six dozen plant shoots and roots had completed the main ingredients.

To break the rock we prefer sharp taps with a hammer, going along the grain or the veining; brute bashing merely splinters into uncontrolled fragments. To set the pattern for the rock to split along a chosen line we sometimes chisel out the line first; often we wrap the rock in a cloth before tapping.

We aim to produce chunky, solid pieces to serve as firm foundations on which to build superstructures. These chunky ones are almost entirely buried right into the sand – certainly not just placed on top – so as to bank the sand back uphill and to hold it there months at a time. Very carefully we choose which is the best face or part to leave exposed, seldom displaying more than one 'aspect' of the chunk – all the rest is to do real work in holding the sand uphill.

Bases Several such chunks of rock form the basis. For instance the glass heater is flat down on tank base, parallel to it, right at the far back and out of sight (not actually touching the glass base or side); the sand there is some 6″ deep or more, and is held back by rocks on either end of the flat heater, imitating Moses as he held back the Red Sea to let his people pass. This 6″ deep canyon, several inches long as it houses the heater tube, can make a lovely cave as it towers up to break sand-level; often we roof it in using a coloured arch-shaped rock gleaming close up to the top lighting. The chunky base of a rock often has a second or even a third rock on it as it tiers vertically up towards the roofing arch. We shape the rocks so that they sit one above the other, often using sand to bed them in the more firmly.

Not only do we slope the sand back-to-front but simultaneously left-to-right.

80 **Arches** Seldom do we put the 'heater arch' merely in the

Right: Fantail Shubunkin. Can stand very cold waters, down to 45°F if necessary, but prefers 62°–68°F (17°–20°C). At home both in the pond and in a tank.

middle. We seek a rhythm, a total pattern; a fussy bit, contrasting with a broad or an open; a delicate with a solid; a flattened with a towering.

Superstructure Additional to the chunky rock is the flat. Slate is an obvious choice, most difficult and most beautiful are the hard rocks that have been coaxed to split into long slabs, say 6″–10″ long and 3″–5″ wide. These we use horizontally, or vertically, one after the other, or alternating, as we bank ever higher and higher – even to break water surface!

Seldom do we leave a bank bare, but tend to 'motif' it: a small ring of coloured stones; an ornament or group thereof, directioned forward, back, or sideways; contrasting colour, with shape or thickness; areas for planting, thickets to hide in; areas for open play and feuding; byewaters for the old, the young and the infirm; main meeting places where life throbs fast down-town in the swirling throng; brightly lit, shaded and

Above: Fantail. Preferences similar to the Oranda's, but hardier and more resistant to cold and crowding as it does not have the lion-mane. Sometimes the finnage can be long and gorgeous.
Left: Shubunkin group.

muted – it is a home for the fish you are building, their home, with as much thought and variation as you would demand in your city and your countryside.

Steps winding upwards look marvellous. Held in place by small flat (vertical) rocks, the steps themselves can taper away to nothing, or lead to a hillside cave; to be coloured, contrasted or plain.

Most effective is rockwork constructed to thicken up to an imposing structure; to slender down and taper, brilliantly to focus gleaming-coloured huge crystal of striking shape or hue.

Colours We use coloured glass chunks and slabs, of course. Lovely crystal knobs, 8″ cube, the raw material from which come those beautifully coloured wine glasses and flower vases that grace your table or your room.

Function The general slope, be it front to rear, or side to side, will be used to hide out of sight, but right out, all functional gadgets like heaters, thermostats, filters, wires, tubes, and what nots. We even make you go round the side to peer at the thermometer. Yet the lie of the land must be such that plants will grow – where the light is – that food debris will naturally fall or be carried by the water eddies to a sensible spot for easy removal. The whole must look good not just for the first week, **83**

Above: Peacock-eyed Sun Bass.
Not peaceful. These are included as
suitable for a coldwater aquarium,
but not for mixing with the friendly
little fish like the Fantails and
Shubunkins. They can definitely nip
tails, and should be kept apart.
Yet they are attractive.
Left: Notropis lutrensis.
Redhorse Minnow. Keeping a pond fish.
such as goldfish, Carp or Orfe, in a tank
is like housing an elephant in an
apartment. 'It lived for months or years'
means it 'endured', when it would have
thrived for a quarter of a century in a
proper pond growing to a full 14".
Pond fish must be given adequate room.
They are fine in a large indoor pond.

but be held firm for a long long time; we allow no gaps through which sand can dribble downhill, to run to a drear waste.

Shade and shelter must be enough; all fish love a 'home' of their own – be it a definable territory, a broad leaf, or, for the fortunate, a cave, a ledge, an overhang, or a cleft, be it of rock or of plants.

Plants We use plants for contrast, and to soften, and to sway; to half hide an entrance or pathway of steps; in lines or clusters; broadleafed or slender; tall or tiny; the odd piece of bark or twig. Seldom do we plant in less than a worthwhile bunch, allowing show-off room for the chosen centrepiece which need not be in front or in the middle but is as likely to be balanced by the heater arch, the main sand-slope, or some other rhythm-pattern.

Result The choice is fabulous. The beauty is stunning. It works. We know – we have done it long and often, in many countries and situations.

Why don't you try? The fish will be the first to thank you; they love varying depths and hollows and have no time for the moaners about 'distracting' from their beauty, or reducing the fish capacity – it's the air surface that governs that.

Aquascaping under difficulties If the tank is relatively too narrow and rather too tall for banking up the sand, then why not insert at the rear a false back, glass, plastic, translucent, clear or opaque; coloured or plain, or patterned. Onto it could be glued with the non-toxic aquarium sealers all sorts of containers for sand-troughs, cups; pockets or beds; arranged in a total V-shape, or diamond shape; or directioned to flow in one way. Heights of 24″ or 36″ thus become beautiful, instead of mere 'empty water' after the bottom 12″.

If the tall tank is wide enough then why not make the false back step forward towards the front in three descents; to give you three levels in reducing height but, say, in increasing widths – so that we end the lower tank with a kind of two-levelled centre area, or a 'roofed over arcade' effect.

Pleasing too can be the 'hanging balcony' effect, not solely at the back but encroaching round to the sides as well if the tank length would welcome it.

Coloured sands can help to give an illusion of width to a too-narrow tank, when arranged in streaks or in linear patterns conjuring an impression of flowing away into the rear distances. We find mirrors rather too 'flick-flick across your eyes' for sustained interest – people tire of them very quickly, except in special situations like the cocktail bar.

Ever used a glass vase? Why not drill the base and mount it on a slightly swaying stand?

Ever used futuristic hoops, coils etc, of fluorescent plastic – in strips, in planes, or in cubes?

How about *underwater* lights – in addition to toplighting – to be soft or strong, to be switched on or off according to mood?

Where do you stop? Where need you! Provided it's non-toxic.

Marine tank layouts These tend to be limited by the struggle to keep them alive and less margin is left for subtle arts and flourishes.

85

Natural method The 'natural balance' method seeks to imitate the ocean shore or shallow creek as far as possible by using local materials. If you are within a car drive of the sea or an estuary, then why not try your luck? Basically the sand from the shore will be kept to minimum depth, even to zero in the feeding areas. See illustration of the tidal pool on page 170.

Collection Collection seems best from the leeward of a reef, or at the time of the receding tide when freshly trapped water and live specimens are found in prime condition. Walking along the receding tide line with your back to the sun helps you to detect the telltale ripple and the glint. Before transporting home any bivalves (cockles or mussels in England, others elsewhere) or anemones it is essential to put them in a small jar of sea water to eject all the filth from their gut. One bivalve dying in the evening can cause a clouded smelly tank by morning. During transport back please don't overcrowd; your specimens will pay for this mistake with their lives. You may need several containers; incidentally, what is their colour? In natural life how often do fish meet a bright red plastic bucket? They get unnerved trapped in an all-surrounding single-coloured glare; and fright or shock can both kill – now or later. Darkness helps, so put a lid on it.

Why neglect to collect the humbler shrimps and crabs etc, as scavengers, or sea-weedy, algae-covered rocks, not to mention anemones which can be prised from underneath with a knife? Maintaining a proportion is essential, giving 'natural enemies' distance to keep away from each other; remembering the needs of the free swimming and the crawling.

Below: Ophiocephalus asiatica. *Chinese Snakehead. 12″. Typical of the many that can 'walk' on land – i.e. get from one drying-up mud pool to another. Jumpers. Predatory.*

All containers must be free of metals and non-toxic; all dying, dead or decomposing things will be removed urgently – preferably before it happens! – and freshly gathered water will be a fine stand-by. The harm one single dead crustacea can do, before you realize that death has occurred, will surprise you; the same goes for the algae-covered rock – greatly appreciated by the fish while alive, but lethal when decomposing. So do use them, but you should ever be on the watch.

Set-up Given these rather dictatorial *do's* and *don'ts* the scope is yours; at the moment no one knows enough to breed marines on a large scale to meet commercial timetables, so there are no true experts, only enthusiasts like yourself. So why not experiment? The next step in progress may easily come from you.

Materials and conditions being local you may not need artificial lights or artificial heating, aeration, etc. Some 'natural method' people scorn such things – yet the ocean is bigger than your tank, and the *constant* eddies and surges are huge scale and are never never ending. Aeration could help. It could also do so during the transport back to the tank and battery-operated air pumps are widely available.

Probably the most important single tip is to put enough light, day and night, on your tank to enable green algae to be established first, all along the sides of your tank. Then start introducing other things. Inside the tank, hiding places and territorial markers are essential. The same applies to caves, dark and protective. If you clean out your tank then these must all be restored *exactly*; imagine how you would feel if *they* suddenly moved your kitchen on the roof and your bed into the garden. It's not décor, but survival.

Yet you must be able to examine and peer enough to spot and remove the dying, not just the dead; including the foods, the droppings, and the refuse 'balls' ejected by the anemones for instance. Anything that can hide the droppings is a hindrance, even an internal filter that collects mulm underneath its curved flanks, and décor has to be strictly functional (for shelter and for pH stability).

Any grey or black spots are highly suspect; grey clouds in the water almost always denote decomposition underneath.

When in doubt, smell it; if it does not actually smell fresh, then assume it's bad.

Dead, grey, black spots on coral can be bleached (using household detergent-free bleach), or just knocked off with a hammer and chisel.

Excess surface scum may be the ejected body mucus of the Lion Fish, for instance, and needs to be skimmed off – frequently.

Shells The coral, the rock, the sea fan, and the red pipe organ coral all can look nice. So too can the shell, if you're sure it's clean and hard. Prudent aquarists refuse point blank to accept any shell as clean unless obviously occupied by its original living owner; hermit crabs that borrow an empty shell are still suspect. The trouble is that dead fragments, shrivelled and dehydrated even for years, come to life in water and start decomposing. You

Below right: Osphronemus gourami. *20″. Indonesia. Large, yet relatively peaceful. Subdued but pleasant colours. Standard preferences, including clean liners and algae.*

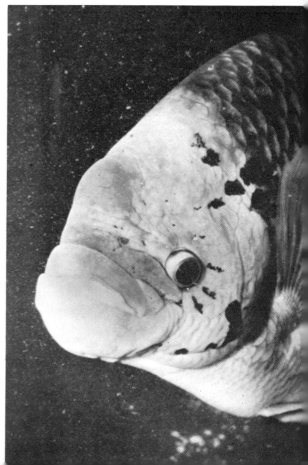

need to soak shells in strong detergent, free from bleach, one to three cupfuls per gallon, turning the shell round and round till all air bubbles have been eliminated particularly from the twisted, inaccessible parts where air might get trapped. After two or three more days, thoroughly rinse and then soak in very strong salt, eight tablespoons per gallon, for a further three days. Finally an ultra-thorough rinse, before use. Even then the prudent aquarist makes periodic checks to see that nothing has drifted in and got trapped.

Artificial shells and china ornaments serve well. Naturally everything is better washed in salt water especially sand whose beneficial micro-organisms could be killed by fresh water. Many people use the sea water again and again, allowing it to settle clear in a dark storage place, and carefully siphoning off the top (see page 50). Please note that the micro-organisms can be killed almost as easily if suddenly washed or flooded by salt water of a different specific gravity; this can be important.

Many an aquarist has such 'natural method' marine tanks that have gone on fine, and many a yarn is (quite truthfully!) told of 'lived for years and never changed the water'.

Other layouts If you are not near the sea, you can still follow the 'natural method' in the sense of keeping simple things in a simple way. A beginner should never be too venturesome; starting small and graduating up, seems to be the best policy.

You'll need artificial salt, and aeration; filters and ozonizers according to taste (and pocket!).

Some people paint the base of the tank with a non-toxic marine aquarium sealer, sprinkle it with $\frac{1}{8}''$ of sand, leave to dry,

Above: Colisa labiosa.
Spawning. Firm old favourites.
Peaceful. Preferences as for the Dwarf Gourami.

Livebearers

Above: Swordtails. Red male. 4″ – 8″.
Right: Albino. 3″ – 7″. There are many
varieties of colours, markings, fins and
tails; lovely in shoals. Hardy and
tolerant of most conditions, although
preferring clean, well-planted areas
alternating with light open waters with
enough room for their restless darts and
swims. Dislike urine saturated tanks
where the ammonia compounds cause
them to go off colour. A change of water
would help. Keep more females than
males, please!
Overleaf: Lebistes reticulatus.
The famous Guppy. 1½″ but now
available in magnificent 4″ or 5″
veil-tailed variations.
Beautiful, peaceful top swimmers.
Hardy, cheap, easy to breed.
As is usual in all livebearers the males are
over attentive and need two females each.

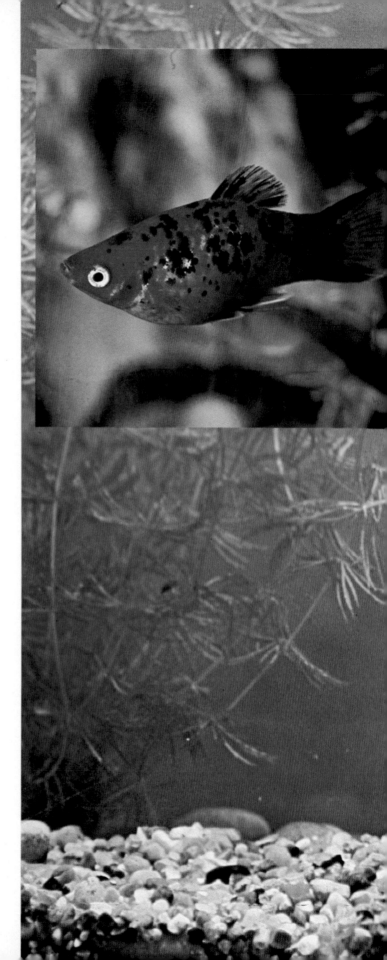

Inset: Tuxedo platy. *4".* *Typical of the many new strains bred by aquarists all over the world. The females, in common with most livebearers, produce several spawnings from a single fertilization; up to 100 babies is not unknown, although 20–40 is usual. Hardy, provided the water is urine-free. Please introduce new stock to prevent excessive in-breeding.*

Right: Mollienisia black. *6".* *Gorgeous, velvet, black. Nervous, they must have privacy or psychological diseases and miscarriages result. The males are virile and need two females. Lyre-tails, sail-fins and speckled are familiar varieties. Vegetarians by preference they should be given varied diets; and appreciate clean, bright, well-planted tanks, urine-free.*

Above: Mollienisia velifera. 6″.
The males of all livebearers have the
pointed gonopodium, normally at rest
parallel to the body; the female anal fin
is short and round. Gestation is from
3–10 weeks depending on season
(summer is quickest) and on the degree
of privacy and freedom from
noise/crowding/dirt.

Left: Xiphophorus variatus.
4″. Swordtails—because the lower part
of the male tail fin is thus elongated —
also, of course, have the pointed
gonopodium; the females having the
short rounded anal fin near the vent.

Above: Xenomystus nigri.
African Knife Fish. 10". Can swim
*forwards or backwards very fast, as is
indicated by the slim back without a
dorsal fin. Obviously crepuscular and
prefers shade. Not to be kept with
smaller fish. Likes live foods, and clean
water. 75°F (24°C), pH 6·6, DH 4.*

Overleaf below: Gnathonemus
macrolepidotus. *Short Nose
Elephant Fish. 8". West Africa.
Typical of this genus which all have
tiny mouths at the end of the 'snout' or
'trunk' through which they suck food,
rather than chew. Almost entirely
defenceless, except that they can emit
mild electric shock, they positively have
to be given a home of their very own,
with more than enough room to go
round, or they squabble. They like
aeration, even though they can cope with
mulm or even mud; the varieties with
clearer markings obviously prefer cleaner
conditions. 77°–84°F (25°–28°C),
pH 6·6, DH 8.*

Overleaf above: Melanotaenia
macculochi. *Dwarf Australian
Rainbow. 6". Typical of the many
rainbow-coloured fish from Australia.
A great favourite. Peaceful; lovely on
shoals. A mid-water scattered spawning
of adhesive eggs; these are a little slow
to hatch (a week or so), and to mature;
as are the young adults to colour up.
Unhurried! But nice when grown.
Hardy, and tolerant of most foods
and conditions. 77°F (25°C),
pH 7·0, DH 8.*

and that's that. Others use an undergravel filter lined with filter wool and then covered by $\frac{1}{2}''$ of marine sand or of crushed coral. Yet others leave most of the base bare, pile the sand or coral round an inverted plastic household funnel fitted with an air line as described in chapter 3.

All three 'work', but arguments rage. For example, many feel that the undergravel filter should fit snugly over the whole area, and have such a good 'grip' at the outer limits that water cannot seep in, except through it; others use probing and radiating under-sand tubes that leave relatively large areas free.

All aim to keep down the hostile bacteria caused by decomposition or by dirt, and to encourage the growth of helpful nitrates, partly by the flow of filtered water, partly by 'correct' pH of around 8·3 (helped by the presence of the crushed coral), and partly by use of the multi-purpose and multi-layered filters discussed in chapter 3. There seems to be growing agreement that more than three layers to a filter is helpful. Increasingly clear is one important fact; you should spend most of your budget on buying equipment (not fish!), the second and the third filters all used simultaneously are far far more advisable than a second or third fish. The time will come, later, when you can add these; the filters come first. This really is important.

Hints to remember Many lay great stress on allowing the helpful micro-organisms to get a grip first; a process that can take two or 12 weeks, and which automatically reduces the level of the hostile nitrates, and stabilizes the pH.

Many insist that algae be grown first, either in the tank itself, or preferably in a separate external filter which is equipped with its own lighting that can stay on constantly; certainly the fish health and appetites are improved with water that has come from algae-saturated waters. Of course, the algae must be maintained and not allowed to start decomposing!

Patience is essential, even a pH reading cannot be taken, after a change, for some 24 hours; the same applies to specific gravity alterations and readings.

The standard rule is to soak everything in salt, first, before use including the filters and their carbon, etc. If you are wiping anything then dip your clean cloth in salt water first, or at least have damp salt on it.

Sudden changes don't help at all. To go from a specific gravity of 1·025 to 1·000 abruptly, e.g. even for washing something, can be lethal to beneficial nitrates. Sudden shock like putting on the tank lights can harm, so always put the room lights on first. Metals must be entirely absent – not in the rocks, lamp clips, wires, etc – plastic coatings being essential.

To get the biggest surface feasible on your aquarium has always been wise advice; with marines the rate of filtration is perhaps even more important – you may need real heavy waves of movement, as in natural life, surging and eddying with evident force.

Temperatures are similar to those for their freshwater cousins, around 75°F (24°C) with room to fluctuate 8°F (4°C) either way. Some fish like the low ranges, some the high; so many factors are involved such as seasons, age of fish, their health, etc. **97**

When in doubt, do as you might for a freshwater tropical fish.

Urine decomposition is aggravated because the lowered oxygen content of the sea water induces a faster intake rate by the fish, with consequent increased urine. If the fish start to breathe faster then you'd better start checking; a part change of water would probably help.

There is no virtue in putting the air pump where it sucks in tobacco or kitchen smells; better to place it out-of-doors on the window ledge and to run in an extra length of plastic air line on the theory that cold is better withstood than tobacco smoke – something an ocean fish has never met before.

For marines it is almost essential to have a separate quarantine tank – this is just one of the facts of life – also a store of ready matured sea water. And, to re-emphasize, that *extra* filter; fitted with that *extra* layer of filter material or chemical, is far more important than having that extra fish. In the end, you and the fish will be much happier.

Introducing fish to the aquarium You know how you truth-

Left: Osphronemus gourami.
Another Giant Gourami from Indonesia.
Right: Trichogaster trichopterus.
Blue, or Three-spot, Gourami.
5". In spite of what some people say, not always peaceful, unless with big fish.

fully feel deep inside, however much you hide it outside, when you are suddenly confronted by strangers all established and assured – and you're just standing about as the newcomer? That's how a fish feels too.

Always feed the established ones first, extra well on this occasion before putting in the new – quietly into the back while the others are feeding in front.

The water temperature, pH and DH should be equalized first; with freshwater fish this necessary precaution tends to be skimped, but you could at least float the fish container in the tank for five minutes to allow the temperatures to equalize. You could, too, take some of the tank water and gently pour it into the container (part emptying this first if necessary) to bring their respective compositions closer together.

The more expensive the fish, possibly the more you'll bother.

Darkness also helps, and the tank can be kept dark for 24–48 hours. The abrupt act of being caught, shoved in a container, jogged about, petrified with the fear of the unknown while trapped in the unfamiliar, all wreaks havoc with the nerves of the fish. Especially is this so with marines, which have almost certainly been caught wild, and have never even met a man before – they seriously can die of fright. Osmo shock. So be gentle and understanding; delayed effects of shock can be very severe. No wonder its gill plates accelerate fifty to the dozen and its increased respiration weakens it.

A useful tip is to retain separately the original water used for transport, and be able to put the fish back into it should they show signs of distress in the (new to them) tank water.

A few petty squabbles for territory are more or less inevitable. Watch out for white spot and other disease.

One further complication applies to marines. The specific gravity of the tank water ought to be altered to that of the fish container! No, it's not a mistake, and should not have been

Left: Helostoma temmincki. *Shoal. The lovable Kissing Gourami. It kisses any fish, plant or rock that it encounters. Hates cold, and must have algae, even green water. Aureomycin medicine works wonders for it.*
Right: Betta splendens. *Red, building nest. Note the bubbles, each wrapped in saliva, to house the eggs. When completed the nest often protrudes 14" above water. Cold draughts and dust are lethal.*

written the other way round. This is where the quarantine tank is so useful. If you can't be bothered to do this, then the plastic bag containing the newcomer should be floated in the tank with some holes punctured in it to allow an interchange of water, and an equalization of the specific gravity. It is essential that the top be kept wide open, or suffocation can happen.

You remember how there were always people firmly entrenched in the best positions when you first entered, smiling bravely? That's what happened to the new fish too – wherever it goes it gets shoved off by the present occupants, and survives or not according to whether it's been given a chance by the omnipotent you. Enough hiding places? Enough territorial demarcations? Enough room?

All fish can be quarrelsome, not just marines or Cichlids; all, too, can bully – and can be scared and hurt and die. **101**

Hence the aquarist, marine or freshwater, is often advised to introduce all the newcomers at once, or, in the case of the marines, *all* the fish that you plan to keep. Then there are no newcomers, and feuds are much less damaging. A little thought, too, in the total harmony of the selection: not merely which type to mix with which, in what numbers; but also with a care for size. Should the species be gregarious then a shoal all the same length looks fine. Should the species be quarrelsome, i.e. frightened and looking for territorial protection, then two fish of the same size are almost bound to challenge each other to eliminate one of them. Putting in a big one and a small one can ensure peace in the quarrelsomes because the big one would not need to prove his strength, and the small would not be expected to challenge – just separate out their spheres of influence. Pattern markings and coloration are a good clue – the more they resemble each other, the more they will fear each other and defend their territories.

Tranquillizers Tranquillizers have long been used during transport of fish. When used to soothe a nervous fish these can be helpful; where used to cram too many in commercial shipments so as to make more money at their expense, then you take your choice – if you're a customer that just wants things cheap, then you'll probably approve. The larger the bag used for transport, the more the fish are pleased.

A famous American tranquillizer now widely available is MS-222 Sandoz, of which one gram dissolved in a pint of water is added to seven gallons of tank water; the fish becoming drowsy, docile and easily caught. This dose is for pH 7·0, DH 8, 75°F (24°C). Too quick a rate of gill breathing is bad, and the dose should be lessened.

Well-known tranquillizers are: 7 per cent carbon dioxide CO_2 gas; Chloral hydrate ($CCl_3 - CHO . H_2O$), dose 10 grams per gallon; Chloretone ($Cl_3 C - C (CH_3)_2 - OH$), dose 1:10,000; Ethyl oxide ($C_2H_5 - O - C_2H_5$), dose $\frac{1}{4}$ oz per gallon; 2-methyl-quinoline, dose 1:200,000.

Top: Swordtail. Red female. 3"–7".
Centre: Xiphophorus variatus.
Pair. 4"–8". Come in many colours.
Standard swordtail preferences.
Hate urine-saturated waters.
Need plants. Like aeration. DH 6–8.

CHAPTER 6
MAINTENANCE
OF THE AQUARIUM

If the earlier chapters have been of genuine help then a trouble-free, easy to run job, should be yours.

Let's first talk of feeding. An enormous choice of dried foods is available world-wide, and enormous has been the improvement on the bread and biscuit crumbs of old.

Food supply Scientifically balanced and methodically produced, in big modern factories, the flake foods have largely ousted the granular, though not entirely. You can get them with protein predominating, or vitamins, or algae, or green-stuffs; to fatten fish, to colour them, to make them breed; single tins, large or small, multiple tins with several kinds housed in separate compartments, or mixed in a multiple form. Food that will float, that will not colour the water, or will emit a special dye to show if you have overfed; made in Denmark, in Germany, in the U.S.A., in Australia, in Japan, in Holland, in England. What a choice! For coldwater fish, for tropicals, for marines; large flakes for hand-feeding; floating pellets to make your fish come to the top to nibble – just about everything.

Yet even these are now being eased out by the newer freeze-dried compounds that remain 'dehydrated' or 'ever-fresh' and come to life in tank water. Back have surged the old old oldies – dried daphnia and ants' eggs; neither of these were of practical use before, being shrivelled husks minus the fleshy parts, but are now relished by the fish as the flesh is 'freshly preserved by freeze-drying'. Also offered are delicacies like tubifex worms or brine shrimps, formerly always difficult to obtain outside the big cities; not to mention liver, fresh shrimp, prawn, crab, and all sorts of (good) mixtures in 'a formula'.

Yet the latest is even more progressive! The new jelly-type foods that don't dissolve but can be left in the tank permanently; the fish nibbling when and how they like. No more overfeeding! These aqua-tabs, tetra-tips, and fish burgers are a real breakthrough.

Feeding Freshwater or marine – you have a choice. And please use it, because fish get fed to the gills with the same food day after day, and long for variety. There is no reason why you should not ring the changes with four or seven tins, one each of the above groups and mixed as to manufacturer and nationality.

The good old rules (except for the latest jelly foods) apply about feeding little and often, and making sure that none falls to rot, all being eaten quickly in two or five minutes. Nor, too, do fish appreciate a slimy scum on the water surface that covers the food with an oily film.

Live foods make a very welcome change, even the garden worm, cleaned and chopped up. Live daphnia and live tubifex worms are sold by us all the year round, in polythene bags containing water, oxygen and food for the daphnia themselves, the unit staying fresh and wholesome for several days – you can now buy a week's supply in one go.

Fresh Norwegian brine shrimp is sealed in plastic containers, rather like the 'freeze-dried', and is marketed all over Australia, the U.S.A., and England.

Choice morsels from your own plate can be offered, cooked or raw, but thoroughly washed so as not to foul the water – meat, liver, shrimp, prawn, roe, cabbage, lettuce, practically anything that does not dissolve too readily. Hung on cotton thread for twenty minutes; you could even have three pieces (different kinds?) on the same thread at top, middle and bottom heights – the Catfish would certainly appreciate your kindness, as would the shy who had been pushed out by the strong if only one feeding pellet or area had been used.

Hints on feeding Most fish are vegetarians, need greens, and rather resent lumps of meat flung at them.

Many a home-loving fish will starve rather than leave its 'home' (and risk losing it to an intruder) and has to be fed there.

Nocturnal fish are well known too.

Please make sure the weak, the bullied and the infirm get some.

If you always feed at the same place, at the same time, and make the same noise, rattle or other 'call sign', you will find your fish waiting there for you. But, there is positively no need always to give the same food.

For baby fish you have liquidized foods like toothpaste, and others for the various stages of growth of the fry to adulthood.

For holidays you have the vacation blocks, slowly dissolving to release fixed amounts per day for a fortnight. And the new jelly-type.

For difficult freshwater fish the hints in the next section on marines can be a real help, slightly adapted.

Feeding marine fish Imagine yourself on the dark side of the Moon, in a shelter built by a totally different form of life, being fed with weird coagulations of a form, texture and taste you'd never conceived of before – that's how your marine fish may feel.

Freshwater fish living in ditches, rivers and lakes have grown accustomed to man; marine fish have not – ocean vastness can scarcely have noticed the occasional ship or swimmer.

Freshwater fish have long been accustomed to feed at the surface; marines have not.

Freshwater fish have long been accustomed to the smell of man, his refuse, his pollution; marines have not.

Relatively clean, vast and flowing in huge waves and tides that no normal river bank could possibly withstand, the ocean teems with plankton, and myriad ever-changing, free growing, foods utterly different from those that you are now offering your pet fish.

Practically any marine fish you see has been caught wild, and abruptly been faced with you. Being on the dark side of the Moon is not a far-fetched analogy – only he didn't ask to come to your tank, you forced him!

So there are no golden rules; large-scale regular commercial breeding is not yet truth; these are the good old days of the individual pioneer when anything goes, and the next technical breakthrough may be due to you.

Remove all food, uneaten after hand feeding, with scrupulous thoroughness, each and every time and use tongs or a siphon tube – your hands could frighten and disturb.

Overfeeding in the sense of surplus scraps littered on the floor does not help at all; each piece should be taken as it falls, in mid-water. Neither does underfeeding help; your patience and time are demanded for this vital job, and *regular* feeding times will soon be noted by your fish.

Feed the tougher fish first, so as to encourage them to allow the others to eat. The carnivorous tend to take food only when it moves; hungry ones follow all moving objects with their eyes, and excitement increases their rate of breathing and the movement of their gill plates.

Feed often. In real life they are accustomed to picking off coral more or less all day, especially the herbivores; in a freshwater tank fish can always turn to the plants, here they rely on you – change the diet very very frequently – as much as you do for yourself. You *must*, just must, spend time on this, each and every single day – as you do on yourself.

Xiphophorus variatus. *Two more of these lovely fish, this time a high fin pair. Beautiful development with striking finnage.*

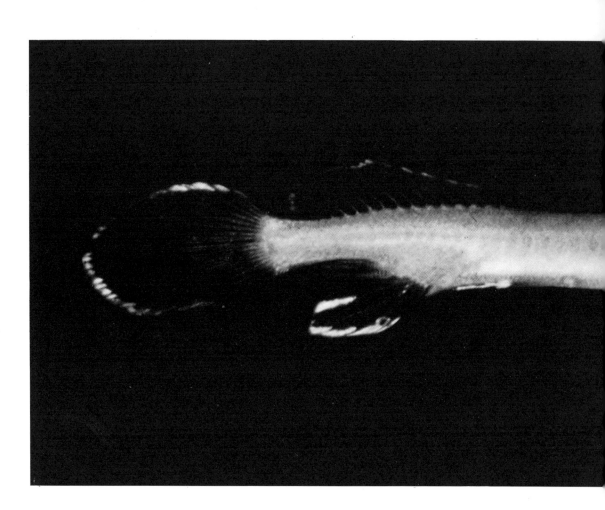

The smaller the mouth, the longer it takes to feed, the daintier the piece and the less the fish will endure the crowded push and shove.

In the ocean the light tends to be poor and fish vision is monocular not binocular like yours, thus the *sound* of food may easily be a greater attraction than sight. Why not hang the morsel on a thread, and dangle it in front? Then you can easily remove it later.

How often does a tropical marine fish in wild life eat an ox, or an oil-cum-fat producing fish like the coldwater cod or halibut? So shred or scrape the beef, the liver, the chicken; keep to flakes of non-oily fish. Daily fresh protein foods are especially beneficial.

Newly hatched shrimps are not all that good; allowed to grow and fill out (e.g. in green algae-rich waters) they are then probably the best we now have to offer. Good, too, are clean, chopped garden worms; Norwegian brine shrimps; lobster, crabs, prawns, mussels and other bivalves that have been thoroughly cleaned in the special way described on page 103. Try and add vitamins like $B1_2$, C and B to the diet or to the water; algae and green foods are a must – lettuce, cabbage, spinach form a vital part of the diet.

Tinned foods in contact with toxic metals are of course lethal. Keeping the cut-up pieces in a fridge seems satisfactory.

Dermogenys pusillus. *The famous live-bearing Half-beak. $2\frac{3}{4}$".*
Malaysia. Surface swimmer and feeder. Great jumper. Hates scum and draughts. Peaceful. Needs plants above water-level for shade, and floating vegetation. Likes clean bright waters, warmer than usual e.g. 80°F (27°C).

Tubifex worms and live daphnia seem to die too quickly in salt to be widely used in the beginning, but are acceptable if readily eaten in mid-water. Mealworms and white worms should be tried.

Coral could be smeared with food and let into the tanks, dangling, or resting on the floor, for half an hour, and then removed till next feeding time. Your fish will soon get to know. With especially slow or shy eaters try this smeared coral at dusk, i.e. at half-light. This applies to nocturnal fish as well.

Try the patented foods, especially the freeze-dried. Try unusual mixtures too like live daphnia that have been allowed to feed in green algae water first, or foods that have been pre-soaked in vitamin additives. If not too cruel, feed live Guppy or molly babies, or adults; for large marines try live goldfish.

Fish 'eat at a gulp', as often as not, so the pieces of food have to be manageable. Anemones need to have the food put directly into their mouths.

A fish already trained to rush for food is a great encouragement to the others; the Sergeant Major and the Beau Gregory are often thus used.

If they maintain a hunger strike past the time when fear should have calmed down and been replaced by hunger, then examine the tank conditions again – urine, pH, DH, temperature, lighting, toxic decay, insufficiently cleaned coral, incom- **107** patible fish so that some are kept off by fear, specific gravity, outside tank noises, flashing lights or movements, more aeration, or less nitrites. A change of water would help.

Don't be discouraged; feeding is probably your biggest single problem. Others have done it; the breakthrough can't be too far off – fish are gluttons and *want to feed!*

Maintaining the tank You may call your specialist dealer to do it; otherwise the following points will help.

Weekly Switch off the aerator. Siphon off the bottom with a length of tubing, or with one of the many gadgets now sold. The object is to get out as much dirt with as little water as possible; one usually holds the tank end of the tube right down over the dirt, $\frac{1}{4}''$ from the sand, sucks it up and then squeezes the tube to inhibit or stop the flow of outgoing water until the tube end is right over the next piece of dirt. Often mulm and dirt collect in patches, according to water eddies; if it's all over the floor, then shame on you! The job should have been done earlier.

Trim the plants. Some will have grown too long or thick; some will have dead leaves, stalky stems, etc. Removal of pitted leaves can become a fetish due to a fear that the 'plant disease will spread'.

Wipe the inside of the tank glass, back and sides; going 'uphill' and not flattening any heaped-up banks of sand. Push the scraper, or your finger, below sand-level to remove the 'dirt-line'– similar to a 'water-line' at the top. If using a cloth, this must be clean and small – a duster would probably be too fluffy, and a handkerchief more appropriate. Pay particular attention to the removal of hard flecks of algae from plastic tanks; please don't let them get a grip.

Check heating; clean filter wools (and carbons?), see that filter tubes are not clogged up (ends and bends especially).

Top up, pouring new water of the same temperature on to a sheet of clean paper or on to a plate held below the water level, so that the incoming flow doesn't stir up the bottom unnecessarily.

By now, with the filter off, any oily scum will have floated to the top, ready for removal. A clean sheet of paper laid flat all over is gently pulled off at water level, not lifted off, so as to skim off the scum like a housewife skims grease off soup. Obstinate little patches in the corners or by the thermostat can be paddled out into the open. Often the skimming is done left to right; then with another sheet of paper, right to left. Really severe cases can be removed with a tumbler (clean!) inserted tail down into the water until its rim is *just* below water level; the inrushing water drags in the scum.

Switch on aerator, make sure the siphon hasn't broken on the filters (i.e. the connecting tubes that must be free of air locks and full of water), feed; relax and smile.

For marines, the removal of uneaten foods is a daily practice, of course; and there are probably no plants. But there may be refuse balls extruded by anemones, and mucus extrusions of fish which will float as surface scum. New water for topping up should match as near the old as possible, including specific gravity.

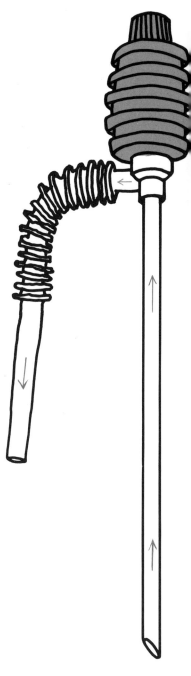

Above: Melanotaenia fluviatilus.
Australian (Pink) Rainbow.
6". Similar preferences to
M. maccullochi.
Right: Bedotia geayi.
Madagascar Minnow. 4".
Very beautiful. Likes high
temperatures 77°–82°F (25°–28°C).
Preferences similar to the Australian
Rainbows, but everything is speeded up
by the higher temperatures. Peaceful.
Top-water feeder. Likes pH 7·2–7·4.
Left: A syphon for cleaning waste
from the bottom of the tank.

Monthly Similar to the weekly routine above, but in addition: Rocks – these will need a brush up; on site, done with your fingers or a cloth; the surface turned to expose a new (cleaner!) face; or removed and scrubbed (no grease or detergent; is the brush clean?). This is better done one rock at a time so as not to disturb the aquascape, and not to let the sand flow down from the banks.

Dark patches round the roots of the plants must be siphoned right out, ruthlessly.

A certain amount of replanting or re-siting of plants may be necessary.

Filter carbons as well as the wools may need renewal. Are there any additional filter layers that need attention, e.g. the chemicals, the peat, or whatever?

Hard flecks of algae on the glass should be scraped off with a finger nail or razor blade. If your tank is of plastic then the weekly or even more frequent cleaning of the plastic front, sides and base must ensure that algae is removed as it forms; otherwise it means using ozonizers or acids (which must not be allowed to harm pH, let alone the fish).

The complete clean-out This is a big job, better done by a specialist, needing several hours and prior assembly of materials and tools.

First the new sand needs to be obtained and cleaned. But cleaned. Wash a little at a time, swilling round with your hands in all the corners, from below up, pouring off the dirty water, replacing with warm or with hot; repeating a dozen or more times, till really clean sand results. As a test, put a little in a (clean) glass, half fill with warm water, shake well, and hold up to the light – if the water is *not* clear, your sand is *not* clean.

What sort of a bucket did you wash the sand in? Any grease or detergent originally in the bucket is now in your sand. Important.

New marine sand or coral can be washed in tap water, no metal in the bucket or any tool for stirring, and then over-soaked in sea water before use. That's for new sand. Washing of used marine sand must, of course, be done in sea water of the *same* specific gravity or all the helpful micro-organisms will be killed.

Have ready plenty of topping up and container buckets, entirely free of household grease or chemicals or detergents, and smelling clean and fresh (not of soap!). You will need enough containers to save the re-usable tank water, apart from those that will house the fish, plenty of cloths, and papers for the floor, where you can spread out the rocks, corals etc, in the same patterns as in the tank layout, for replacement in the same way. Vital is this point if you have quarrelsome fish like marines or Cichlids, who have firmly staked out claims – for them the restored territorial demarcations must be identical with the old; similar will not do. Got enough other containers to wash the dirty rocks in? Nets for catching the fish, new carbons, wools and so forth for your filters, more plants, tools, siphons, new heaters, covers for the temporary fish containers in case fright makes them jump out, spare containers (clean) for the weak or

Top: Pantodon buchholzi. *Butterfly Fish. 5". West Africa. A great jumper. Needs clean, clear waters of 78°–85° F (26°–30° C). Right:* Badis badis. 3½". India. *Changes colour according to surroundings because its family are hunters. But this type is peaceful enough. Likes shoals and shelter. Great eater, especially live foods. Likes shade alternating with light. 77°–84° F (25°–28° C), ph 6·8–7·2, DH 8–10. Far right:* Toxotes jaculator. *Archer fish.*

quarrelsome fish – all should be there and ready, before you start. Have your tea break, and be ready to do a start-to-finish job.

Count the difficult-to-catch things like eels, sucking Catfish, etc, also the small and the easily overlooked.

Without disturbing the tank, switch off the heating and filtration, but not the lighting, and siphon off to keep as much of the old water as is clean and re-usable.

Next remove the plants, gently rinsing them under a warm tap, pruning, and laying them in rows (roots all facing one way) ready for replanting. Keep them damp – and somewhere you won't crush them by mistake.

Remove rocks, singly; scrub in hot water (is the brush clean?) or in identical sea water if for marines. Arrange on the prepared floor in the same pattern as in the tank. Bleaching of corals cannot be done now; this will have to be a separate job.

Remove heaters, internal filters, etc (but not the undergravel one), and clean them ready for re-use.

By now the remaining tank water will be a ghastly mess; siphon off all but two or three inches, or more if your fish are big, leaving just enough to keep them wet. It should now be easy to catch them. You have already noted the difficult ones, provided separated homes for the weak and the quarrelsome, and covers to prevent jumping.

Fish gone, please resist the temptation to pick up and empty the tank (unless it is injection moulded plastic in one piece) because of the real danger of leaks (discussed in chapter 1) when

Datnoides microlepis. *Typical of the many new African fish now coming onto the market. Large. Beware of its mouth. Keep warm.*

the retaining water pressure is removed and the glass tends to spring away from the frame.

Mop out and clean as quickly as feasible, putting absolutely no pressure whatsoever on the outside of the glass; this will be wiped when the tank is full again. Remove all the sand, under-gravel filter, water; all out.

Now replace as promptly as you can the cleaned undergravel filter, the washed sand, the heaters (flat and low), the rocks and corals, all the internal gadgets hidden, sand gloriously banked as per the previous chapter; add water some 5°F (2°–3°C) warmer than usual to heat up the sand and other contents, re-using as much of the saved water as prudent, till the tank is 10 per cent short of full having allowed for the water now housing the fish, if you are replacing this too.

Replant the plants in nice bunches (see chapter 5).

Add the fish; temperature equalized?

Top up, checking temperature and specific gravity. Skim off surface scum; feed.

Relax and smile, not having forgotten to switch the heating on. Have well-earned tea break.

Nervous, old or weak fish may suffer; this can be helped by both catching and replacing them first, meanwhile housing them separately; most survive quite well. It would be practical to keep an eye open for sores, disease, frayed fins, etc, during the days following.

Tools are best kept separate, and free from kitchen, paint or other smells. A cloth used for household dusting or polishing and then dipped or flicked over the tank can wreak havoc, as can detergents or household grease in the topping-up bucket. It's amazing how far odours can travel; before you use it in your **112** fish tank make sure it smells fresh.

Cichlids

Symphysodon aquifasciata axelrodi. 5". Amazon. The 'queen of the aquarium' and the most prized of the freshwater beauties. The tank will have to be large, clean, well aerated, bacteria-free, and planted. Also it must provide crevices and caves for privacy, and the water should be soft, acidic and warm. The food must be dainty and varied, and include live foods. Shoaling helps; isolation does not. Breeding is easy if the water is right: 76°–84°F (24°–29°C), pH 6·0–6·6, DH 2–4, a. ast 15" deep.

Left: Symphysodon aquifasciata axelrodi. *Two more of these beauties. To identify the sexes notice that the male anal fin is more pointed at the end towards the tail, as are the genital papillae; the ventral fins are crescent-shaped; the head is often more bull-like, with a deepening of colours at top, immediate back, and in the fins; he is usually larger too. The female genital papillae are cone-shaped, and her ventral fins fall in an S-curve. Colours vary widely.*

Below: Cichlasoma severum. *8". Guyana. A larger relative of C.* meeki *(see page 118), they become more pugnacious as they grow older. Like light/shade contrast, and are mostly carnivorous but do eat algae too. Courtship is tough, with locked jaws and real pulls of strength; protect the female if necessary and remove both parents when fry are free-swimming (about 5–10 days including hatching) although they are solicitous guardians till then.*

Above and left: Pterophyllum
scalare. *6½". Amazon. Loves shoals.
Males have the anal fin sharply angled
from the body; pointed genital papillae,
angled backwards; the lower jaw tends
to protrude; the body is slightly more
circular than the female's and a strong
light shone sideways through it shows a
flat topped intestine with a hollow
depression in it, the female one being
rounded. In the male the distance between
the ventral and the anal fin is greater
and is straight lined. Viewed head on
the female body is more full behind
and below the pectorals.
Eggs hatch in 48 hours. 75°F (24°C),
pH 6·8–7·0, DH 8.*

Above: Cichlasoma meeki.
*Firemouth. 5″. Yucatan. Almost
peaceful, these large tough fish have
become more popular as people keep
additional tanks. Often too quarrelsome
to be kept with others, or even with their
own kind, unless in suited pairs.
They are just as rough with plants
and tank furnishings – including
tubes for the heater or whatever. Hefty
eaters including green foods rather
surprisingly. They stand most
conditions, yet need filtration if
only because of their own excreta.
The Firemouth can be kept with other
big fish, otherwise their preferences are
standard. 74°–77°F (23°–25°C),*
118   *pH 6·8–7·2, HD 10–14.*

Right: Astronotus ocellatus.
*Oscar or Marble Cichlid. 6″.
Venezuela. Scales are invisible so that
a body mucus coating like firm velvet
is featured. Not too quarrelsome.
Hearty eater.*

Right: Crenicichla saxatilis.
Ring-tailed Pike Cichlid. 12".
West Indies. Very pugnacious,
but beautiful. Does not uproot plants
and likes their shelter. 68°–72° F.
(20°–22° C). Needs aeration.
Below: Herrichthys cyanoguttatus.
Texas Cichlid. 12". Stands low
temperatures 68°–70° F (20°–21° C),
but fouls the water quickly with heavy
body slime and excreta, so please give
really big tanks, aeration and filtration.
Pugnacious, and likes to have a clear
all-round view of things – anything in
the way gets moved.
Far right: Aequidens maroni.
Keyhole Cichlid. 4". Venezuela.
Peaceful, even timid, and needs a home
of its own, like a clump of plants.
Omnivorous, so include algae.
75°–82° F (24°–28° C), pH 6·8,
DH 8.

Left: Geophagus jurupari.
*Earth-eater. 10". Brazil. Peaceful with
fish of its own size. Its tank must
contain very soft sand or silt as the fish
actually shovels up and even ejects some
via the gills! Be that accurate or poetic
this fish certainly stirs up the bottom.
Does not uproot plants unduly, and eats
green foods. May be a mouth breeder,
i.e. house the eggs in its mouth for
hatching; as do the Tilapia also
illustrated.*

Left: Tilapia mossambica. 7".
*East Africa. Mouth-breeder.
Not too peaceful.*

Right: Etroplus suratensis.
*Green Chromide. 14". Ceylon.
Prefers brackish waters when its colours
shine forth. Hardy. Can be left with
fish that are nearly its own size.*

Catfish family, loaches, etc.

Above: Kryptopterus bicirrhis.
*Glass Catfish. 5". India. A great
favourite. Loves clean bright mid-waters
where it shelters under a broad leaf,
its long feelers held quivering forwards
to warn of danger or of food.
Very short-sighted. Loves warmth;
obviously defensive, liking the
comfortable security of a shoal;
would greatly appreciate a 'group
shelter', e.g. cave, plant thicket of heavy
outgrowing leaves in midwaters;
the whole shoal would concentrate there.
Looks fabulous in strong angled light,
not just overhead. Completely transparent
– even the green of the leaf is showing
through. Dainty feeder, liking
greens but mostly insects or their
substitutes like daphnia and tubifex
worms. 76°–83°F (25°–29°C),
pH 7·0, DH 6–10.*
Left: Botia lohachata. *Pakistan
Loach. 5". Multi-barbled mouth of a
greedy feeder (hence not too peaceful),
smudged markings or murky water
scavenger. Must have hiding places,
like most Loaches.
77°F (25°C), pH 7·0, DH 8.*

Below: Etropiella debauni. $3\frac{1}{2}''$.
*Congo. Blue, sort of 'Glass Cat fish'.
Similar preferences. Not quite so
short-sighted, but still needs protection,
e.g. in a shoal; and, again, dim oblique
lighting preferred.*

Left: Callichthys callichthys.
Armoured Catfish. 8". Brazil.
Preferences as for the crepuscular
H. plecostomus *and other wide-spaced*
eye bottom dwellers. Its auxiliary
breathing apparatus has been evolved to
cope with murky waters (look at its
dark and smudged colouring) and it has
become a bubble – nest builder (see
Betta splendens *on page 101). To be*
kept only with fish of its own size.

Below: Hypostomus plecostomus.
12". Brazil. Typical of the many with
strong sucker mouths, which can grip
tenaciously in the strongest currents –
hence fast filtered clean waters are
essential. It eats enormous quantities
of algae and other vegetarian foods,
so needs brightly lit tanks; tends to
be crepuscular and must have shade
in which to sleep during the day.
Peaceful. A great favourite. 74°–77°F
(23°–25°C), pH 7·0, DH 8.
Filtered!

Labeo bicolor. *Red-tailed Black Shark.*
7". Thailand. Peaceful, timid, algae
eater, gregarious. Preferences as for the
128 *Flying Fox. Its larger cousin the Black*

*Shark (*Morulius chrysophekadion*) is*
too snappy and big for fish smaller than
itself. Clean, aerated, bright waters.
78°F (25°C), pH 6·8, DH 6.

CHAPTER 7
DISEASES

First, why did they fall sick? Had you given them an unsuitable layout? Next, had you made a mistake in maintenance? Last, what is the disease and the medicine? This chapter will, therefore, be arranged in these three sections, and in that order.

Tank layout in relation to body shapes and markings
Fish will always talk to an intelligent and compassionate owner, explaining their preferences and their needs. A little intuitive understanding of the body shapes, of their colours and markings, of their mouths and eyes, of their fins, and you can have the whole story if only you have eyes to see and ears to hear. This theme began to be developed by me in earlier books and in Pelham's *Beginner's Guide to Tropical Fish* the example of the Dwarf Gourami (*Colisa lalia* illustrated here on page 70) was elaborated; the fish itself is so beautiful and so popular, yet some aquarists have unnecessary difficulty maintaining its gorgeous colours. So let us consider it in detail.

The body is flat, laterally compressed, clumsy and no use for attack. It is ideal for sheltering in a cleft or crevice.

The feelers are long and graceful, the mouth is small and dainty. Both preclude attack. They suggest shoaling for defence and for group self-confidence. The dainty mouth stops it being a scavenger; it is more likely to be fastidious, as is also indicated by the long feelers. It probably dislikes dirt.

The high colours of the body, in fabulous mosaic of delicate reds, blues and greens, would make it far too vulnerable unless camouflaged (since it is not equipped to attack or to fight). Hence its home waters are almost certain to be brightly lit by strong sun streaking through overgrowing vegetation piercing the water in alternating light and dark rays – a perfect protection for the high-coloured body.

The eyes are clear and bright; added to the dainty mouth and the body colouration it is obvious that the waters are clear. They would have to be flowing too, or else the bright sun would make sluggish waters too green. There is no suction pad (in the mouth, or body) for hanging on in strong currents, so the waters should flow gently; and not be too deep as the shape of the body is laterally compressed, not circular like deepwater loving fish.

If the waters flow gently, in strong light, through overgrowing vegetation, then plenty of greenstuffs would be available, and its dainty mouth confirms its preference for green foods; a vegetarian diet. Such waters often are soft, DH 4–8, slightly acid, pH 6·8, and warm.

129

The mouth is terminal (not pointing up or down but forward); so it's a mid-water inhabitant.

In fact the home waters in Malaysia are exactly as the fish has just described to us: small streams, clean, gently flowing, 80°F (27°C), pH 6·8, DH 4–8, shallow, bright light piercing the overgrowth, plenty of green lush foods. The fish live in protective shoals, in reeds and rock crevices.

Without aeration, with no clefts to hide in, no protection from the tank top light, dirty, crowded and wilting in its lone shyness, fed on meat or worms – no wonder it falls sick! Rather than medicines when sick, you give it a clean tank, 9″–12″ deep, nicely planted and aerated, with the aquascape supplying crevices, clefts, tall *Vallisneria* reed-like plants, temperature 80°F (27°C), say six or twelve in a shoal and you'll be transfixed by their beauty. Sensitive and responsive – they'll soon get to know you personally.

Now that this idea of fish preferences has been understood, the excuse of the insensitive brute of an owner, who neither sees nor hears but just slaps in medicine, is far less valid. Let us look further:

A body long, slim and torpedo-shaped clearly suggests a fast far-reaching swimmer who wants space to roam – open waters in fact. If the fins tend to clumsiness or to over-growth, then darting, fast acceleration may be the keynote.

Light sheening on the body, and longitudinal streaks, indicate love of clear waters and ability to swim against the current.

So do clear, bright eyes that seem to have wide fields of vision. Often red (or other colour) rimmed.

The well-loved Zebra Danio is a good example of a sheeny torpedo body – with clear longitudinal stripes, good fins, clear red-rimmed eyes – that swims fast and far constantly on the search for food, needing frequent feedings (it has short digestive intestines and eliminates quickly), loving to dash upstream against the flow of aeration bubbles or filter jets.

High body colouring as on the Dwarf Gourami, the Neon Tetra and the Cardinal Tetra denote a preference for the piercing sunlight already described. But heavy bars as on the Tiger Barb denote less overgrown vegetation, allowing sunlight through more in broad blotches than in thin streaks. Which blotch will the fish choose – shade or sun? The clear, red-rimmed eyes of the Barb shows preference for sun; its barbels at the terminal to sub-terminal mouth show greed and a tendency to forage – hence it will eat anything. Its teeth denote its love of eating flesh.

Terminal, supra-terminal and sub-terminal are the three main mouth divisions; hence mid, upper and lower water dwellers.

Scats are greedy scavengers, always hungry. Look at their mouths. Their untidy body pattern of dots, haphazard and dark, show that they will stand murky waters of almost any type – they are found both in brackish and in fresh waters as they scrounge round the estuaries.

Their round bodies denote ability to live in deep waters. They lack feelers, which added to their random spots means a

Above: Pterophyllum scalare. Marble. One of the many new types. Beautifully shaded marking. Hardy and peaceful.
Below: Cichlasoma festivum. 6″. Guyana. Less pugnacious than C. severum, and a well-known favourite.

lack of fastidiousness – they'll go anywhere, any water, and eat anything.

Angels won't. Look at their sheeny, clean bodies with clear-cut bars and bright red-rimmed eyes; look too at those graceful long feelers. Anything won't do. The water has to be clear, bright and clean. Mid-water terminal mouths. Good finnage, suitable for a darting not for a steady swim; but all-in-all (body, mouth, markings and fins) able to hold its own – though not much more, for a relatively big fish – hence would appreciate the safety of a shoal. Obviously needs tall reeds and crevices, but equally obviously able to sally out into open waters. Not a stay-at-home.

Hatchets with their compressed lower bodies, horizontally flattened tops, and huge pectoral (breast) fins are obviously jumpers. Supra-terminal mouths confirm their love of top waters, as do good eyes for seeing. They could not be happy unless provided with *top* floating weeds, reeds, twigs and so forth. Their body sheen is bright, their markings are clean-cut (look at the Marble Hatchet) so they would have to have clear bright warm waters. Make them cold, and expect them to catch white spot disease.

The more the back is arched the slower the swim; add a sub-terminal mouth and you have a bottom-dweller like a Catfish.

Above: Tilapia melanopleura. *17″. Congo. Mouth-breeder. Can be kept with fish of its own size when small – i.e. up to 5″.*
Right: Pelmatochromis thomasi. *Arnold's Cichlid. 4″. River Niger. Quarrelsome, in spite of its small size. Must have a home of its own, clearly staked out, which it will guard but seldom leave.*

Note the flat tummy – right down to the very tank base the fish goes. Note too that the colour of the tummy is lighter than its back – obviously to keep to the bottom.

If the back (still darker than the tummy) has clearer markings on it, like the Leopard Catfish, then obviously the waters must be cleaner and brighter than those denoted by the dull colour of the Aneus Catfish – which can survive mud and mulm the Leopard Catfish could not, as further stressed by its eyes which are brighter too.

Look at the Upside-down Catfish which shrieks its preferences at you – an overhanging ledge along the underneath of which it can suck. The big suction pad mouth to hang on with, the small wide-spaced eyes, the hollow tummy (not merely flat) and the arched back.

Bright body markings plus the suction mouth denote sunlight plus strong currents of flowing waters. Hence clear clean aerated tanks.

Such are some of the main points our fish are only too anxious to communicate to us, so that we can understand them, and not cause them to fall sick through our carelessness or our ignorance. With marine fish too, this intuitive approach will be found helpful. Many a sickness can be prevented by attention to layout.

133

Sickness In a sense this whole book has been an attempt to prevent sickness and to aid health, and it might be useful to group here the hints scattered throughout the earlier pages.

With a sick fish, it might be worthwhile first to read about it (or similar ones) as detailed in the captions or the next chapter, then to focus on this section as a whole and try to sense or find the cause – and thus the cure.

Did you buy from a specialist dealer, who really knows fish, and does not spread his time over all manner of other livestock? After all, the general knowledge of a garage 'handy-with-cars' man is of little applied use in building an orbiting space ship – you need a *specialist*, one who concentrates on fish, and therefore has a chance of keeping up to date in this ever moving industry.

Does he love his fish, keep up with the latest medicines, keep his tanks nice, have warmed wrapping-up paper handy, and plenty of catching nets; does he try to stop spread of disease, and in general have a good atmosphere? Or is he in it just for the money!

Yet with ever growing imports, new diseases inevitably are introduced, and at a faster rate than man's knowledge grows. In addition man does stupid things with his planet; take for instance atomic radiation – the radiation from the so-called peaceful uses of nuclear power units is every bit as harmful as that from a bomb, and is gradually permeating our bodies. Burying nuclear waste in lead-cum-concrete in the sea leads to seepage after 10–15 years – and the first refuse was dumped in 1943. This dangerous seepage does not spread evenly over the vast gallonage of the ocean but tends to concentrate on sea growths like seaweed, which washes our shores and is used in commerce. And it gets into the bones of fish. Look at the well-known disease of white spot. Originally there were only two kinds, and for years and years that was all. Now there are six, at least, different 'mutations', some of which are extremely difficult to control. The disease is now found among the open waters of Africa, Asia, Latin America and parts of Europe; simply taking a fish from one tank and immediately putting it in an identical tank (and water) alongside can of itself bring out the latent white spot!

However, we must continue to do our best to prevent disease.

Did you equalize the temperature before putting the fish in (pages 97–98)?

How about pH (page 30), DH (page 30) and specific gravity (page 49)?

How about the nitrite level and decomposition?

How about the water in the tank (page 52)?

How about urine in the tank (page 28)?

How about tank layout and hiding places (page 101) or shade?

How about changes of food (page 103)?

How about the proportion and vigour of the plants (page 61)?

How about the hidden dirt in the undergravel filter?

How about black patches at the plant roots (page 57)?

All these could result in the fish becoming discoloured, being listless, drooping the fins (or in the case of some fish like the

Etroplus maculatus.
Orange Chromide. 3″. Ceylon.
Lovely. Peaceful. Happiest with
a shoal, in a home of its own.
Likes plants.

marines holding them ultra-stiff in an unnatural rigidity),
splintering off into isolation, hiding unduly, hanging head
down, trying to escape into a protective clump or coral, trying
to bury head down into the sand, accelerated breathing, and
inflammation of the gills.

All these mean 'poisoned water'; something is wrong and a
change in whole or part is urgently required.

Is the filter saturated (page 30)?

Less violent symptoms are hunger-strikes, body marks or
blemishes, and ragged fins.

White precipitate on the plants (page 57), plants that straggle
too much, unusual bubbles in the tank or on the surface are all
signs for you to investigate.

Scum on top (page 108)? Toxic substances or metals?

Fumes from the air pump (page 98)?

Temperature stratification (page 37)?

Smelly tools or cloths used? Been kept in a place near smells? Sure?

If the fish mouth stays open too long, and especially if its rate of breathing increases, let alone if body sores erupt, then it has an internal disease and your dealer (specialist!) will advise – perhaps a drug like phenexothol is the answer. You can always feed foods soaked in medicine to the fish.

Medicines Increasingly the medical industry is coming to the aid of the aquarist and really sophisticated medicines, with drugs, antibiotics, vitamins and so forth now widely marketed. So much so that many people rely on them heavily.

In part because of this, and also because the average aquarist does not have the facilities to bother overmuch with scientific jargon and finesse, we propose to adopt the groupings first made in Pelham's *Encyclopaedia of Tropical Fish* and which have now proved popular. In brief the main diseases of white spot, fungus

Left and right: Corydoras aeneus. *3". Venezuela. The good old oldie. Peaceful, hardworking and hardy. Breeding is easy. Note the saucy wink of its eye.*

and Oodinium are detailed; the rest are put in groups, with little attempt to sub-divide between coldwater, tropical and marine, the more easily to enable recognition of the type of medicine required.

Always, but always, it is wise to feel one's way, and to administer doses gradually by drip or in several stages, spaced hours or even a day apart; so many factors can vary to make a 'normal' dose harmful in particular cases. Dim light helps, dirt doesn't. A 2°F (1°C) variation may. Algae may die and decompose.

Should you have an ozonizer or an ultra-violet ray light you will find both to be most helpful. Many keep them on practically all the time at a low rate, others preferring shorter or longer bursts of varying strength. Certainly they will disinfect your tank.

Dropsy Dropsy is when the scales all stick out and the fish becomes bloated – in patches, or all over the body. Nowadays it is nearly always due to an internal infection and medicines are available – so too is the tip of soaking foods in medicines before feeding.

The disease is not normally infectious unless the skin breaks and the causative micro-organisms escape into the water; there are many many kinds of these now. Lower temperatures slow down their life cycle, as you would expect. **137**

The following could help: oxytetracycline or chloromycetin (30 to 90 milligrams per gallon, in three doses); aureomycin (2 grams per gallon); para-chlorophenoxethol using 50 cc of a stock solution (made by mixing one part with 100 parts of water) per gallon; times and methods as under *Fungus* below. Or these can all be fed to the fish in foods soaked in 1 milligram for 10 grams of fish food.

As new strains come along you can always try mixing the medicines in the hope that the fish will prove tougher than the micro-organism and will therefore survive the extra strain of, say, adding quinine dihydrochloride to the phenoxethol, doses as detailed below under *White spot*. Or try new ones like the equally drastic para-chlorophenoxethol (200 cc from a stock solution of 0·1 per cent per gallon).

Well known is the remedy of puncturing the swollen parts to release the exudation – insert a needle a few millimetres before the anal and in the direction of the head.

Eye swelling Eye swelling, or Exophthalmus, is swelling behind the eyes that can end by pushing them out of their sockets;

Synodontis angelicus.
Another Upside-down Catfish.
10″. From West Africa.
Relatively new. Large. Almost entirely crepuscular, i.e. dusk, dawn and night mover.

many variations, especially with marines. The cause can be sheer nerves (yes!), virus, bacteria, or even too many too-fine oxygen bubbles with or without O_3.

An external brushing with a 2 per cent solution of silver nitrate may help, plus a second brush with 2 per cent potassium dichromate; followed by a three-day bath in a solution of 1 gram potassium dichromate per 5 gallons, adding $\frac{1}{2}$ oz rock salt as well.

The lesser of two evils may be to sacrifice one eye by using a hypodermic syringe, but you could also try the medicines suggested for fungus – either as liquids or as foods saturated in them. A hit-or-miss attempt could also be a seven-day bath in potassium antimonyl tartrate, 1 grain per gallon, plus food soaked in phenoxethol; even adding 30 cc per gallon of 1 per cent solution of phenoxethol to the bath.

Alternatively the bath can be in a sulphamerazine sodium, 4 grains per gallon.

Body swelling and flukes The sign of flukes is when the fish rub themselves against anything that is handy. Unless marks caused by an external blow, for which a simple swabbing (as for eyes) or mild disinfectant may be enough, these are caused by internal disorders and should be treated as under *Fungus*. A purist may groan at these sweeping groupings of disease, but the average aquarist may find they work. If that fails try the white spot baths.

Lice and worms These are parasites clinging externally to the body, and can be pulled off by tweezers, although the real harm will have been done not to the body, not even to the eyes, but to the ultra sensitive gill plates. If these are inflamed then cures get more despairing.

First a swabbing or a very quick dip of 2–6 minutes in ordinary cooking salt can be done (strength 4 teaspoons per quart); or a bath in potassium permanganate ($\frac{1}{4}$ grain per gallon), or both.

Next a bath in gammexane (1 cc per 20 gallons, of a stock solution of 1 per cent) for a week.

More drastic still is a five-minute immersion in household ammonia, mix 10 per cent with 90 per cent water, from this stock solution add 30 cc per gallon, followed by a bath in methylene blue (dose as under *White spot*).

Formaldehyde can also be used. A 1 per cent solution from which 20 cc are added per gallon; after 3 days, add another 10 cc per gallon, and yet again after 6 days. After 10 days all the water should be changed. Some people also add further ingredients to this bath like quinine, methylene blue or mepacrine hydrochloride.

The remarks at the beginning of the section about feeling one's way, and of increasing doses (or mixtures) in cautious stages, all apply. The truth is that sporozoans vary almost every time, every import, and hit-or-miss *at once* is often better than long delays getting accurate analysis with sophisticated equipment which few of us have outside major hospitals.

Red spots and marks respond to sulphanilamide, sulphadiazine, or sulphamerazine in doses of $\frac{1}{2}$ gram per gallon for 3 days, increasing by 25 per cent for another 3 days, and by a final

25 per cent for the last 3 days. Water should be changed after 10 days.

See also treatment and doses under *White spot*, below; they are worth a try.

Fungus In the old old days 'you only got it on goldfish', now you get it on everything including marines. In the old old days you said it was dermatomycosis, now it can be almost anything. Note that many of the parasites are not obligatory, i.e. they can live on without the presence of fish so that even your carefully-stored-in-the-dark-and-filtered water may have it! Yet healthy fish seldom get it, or recover rapidly if they do, so you don't have to disinfect the aquarium with any degree of fanaticism after an outbreak, nor need you worry unduly. Some suggested cures:

Swab with iodine, with mercurochrome or with merthiolate, all diluted 1,000 times – i.e. 1 cc in a litre of water. There is no harm in wiping the affected parts with more than one of the above – any harm is likely to be in the catching and handling of the fish, not in the chemicals, so you may as well try a couple. Also dichromate of potash, diluted 100 times. A small paint-brush is as good a swab as any. A bath in mild acriflavine, or methylene blue, or salt, etc, would be prudent.

A bath of approximately 10 days usually kills off the sporo-zoans. The doses, being added in two or three stages with or without partial changes of water, could be given with the following:

Potassium dichromate, $2\frac{1}{2}$ grains per gallon;

Phenoxethol. Make with distilled water a stock solution of 1 cc to 100 cc of water; from this you can give 40, 60 or even 100 cc per gallon;

Malachite green, the new wonder, instant, drug. Overdoses can be fatal; try $\frac{1}{4}$ grain per gallon;

Terramycin in doses from 50 to 250 milligrams per gallon, building up the dose in three stages;

Parachlorometaxylenol dissolved with four parts of water, and from this stock solution use 10, 20, 40 or 60 cc per gallon;

Chloromycetin, 20 to 90 milligrams per gallon; or

Aureomycin, 2 grams per gallon, and sulphamerazine sodium, 4 grains per gallon, can all be tried singly, with salt, or in combination.

A drastic dip would be 5 to 10 minutes in a 3 per cent solution of commercial hydrogen peroxide, diluted with six parts of water.

A milder form of treatment is methylene blue – enough to turn the water from light to dark blue, stopping short of purple. Some people add 2 teaspoons of cooking salt per gallon as well.

If you wish, in despair, radically to increase the dosage, then it can help to drip in the medicine over whatever period of time you have allocated – 5 minutes, or 2 hours.

Immersing fish for limited periods like this is often done by leaving them in the catching net which is then spread out in medicine, and simply pulling them out at the end of the timed period, or before if they keel over in distress as they may easily do if weak beforehand, or if other chemicals are present in the water.

Try dosing food with the medicine before feeding. Keep in dim light. Aerate. Permit no dirt. No algae.

White spot Tiny white dots on (not in) the fish, perhaps on the fins first, the size of a pinpoint to pin head, depending on which of the six types it is (please see page 134).

Now inborn in the wild fish of more than half our planet; quarantine is virtually impossible as it can reappear any time. As already stated the very act of taking the fish from one tank and putting it straightaway into another identically conditioned tank, can bring out the white spot – within hours or a day depending on type.

The old cure was to raise the temperature to 90–95°F (32°–35°C); but the local temperatures in Asia and Africa are already that.

We now suggest that you seesaw the temperature: 80°F (27°C) one day, 95°F (35°C) the next, back to 80°F (27°C) on the third, and so on. This brings a gasp of dismay; every book says it's wrong, my earliest ones included – but it works.

Or you can use the ultra-strong wonder drugs like Malachite green ($\frac{1}{4}$ grain per gallon) when you don't need to alter the temperature at all. A whole range of 'instant' cures are now marketed based on this and on controlled copper poisoning. Drastic, but effective for the present range of known parasitic cysts.

More orthodox medicines, normally coupled with raising the temperature 10°F (6°C) include:

Methylene blue, which turns the water dark blue, but just short of purple. Best medical quality. Dirt does not help, dark-

Epalzeorhynchus siamensis. *Flying Fox. 7″. Thailand. Similar preferences to its cousin,* E. kallopterus, *but even more peaceful and hardworking. Likes algae, of course.*

ness does. Don't worry if you can't see the fish for a week in the blue medicine. Plants will survive, usually. Aeration helps. Has least side effects, but takes longest to cure, e.g. 10–15 days.

Quinine hydrochloride, 1 gram for 20 gallons.

Mepacrine hydrochloride, more drastic, $\frac{1}{4}$ grain per gallon.

Mercurochrome, 1 per cent solution from which add 3 or 4 drops to each gallon of tank water.

Neutral acriflavine or aureomycin. One milligram (0·46 grain) dissolved in 100 cc of water, and from this stock solution add 10 cc per gallon to the tank.

To repeat, all baths are better given with the medicine added in stages separated by 2–3 days; some aquarists change a half or a third of the water at the same time so that the second and third have to be proportionately increased to allow for the dilution of the new water.

Invariably all the water is changed when the bath is over.

If your tank is dirty and liable to cloud, then the aeration can start halfway up the tank, leaving the base undisturbed. What your Catfish would say about this is not too clear.

Dim light, live foods, and even the addition of cooking (not table) salt and even of other chemicals can be tried.

The higher the temperature, the more the life cycle of the cyst is speeded till it reaches the vulnerable free-floating stage when it will die if it does not find a host.

An ozonizer would be an enormous help.

Oodinium Oodinium, or Velvet Disease, is the built-in disease of the marines and strongly resembles the white spot of fresh-

water tropicals except that it has a pale yellow colour. A dino-flagellate, this causative organism is also best attacked in the free-swimming stage, after the parent cyst fragments. Unfortunately it can reproduce even when still on the fish skin. Always present.

Copper poisoning is the main method of attack because the resulting irritation causes skin mucus to be exuded to dislodge the cyst. Many patented medicines are sold; the aquarist would be advised to stick to them rather than try to make his own, unless he is a chemist of course. Twenty milligrams per gallon of copper sulphate would be the strongest advisable dose.

Darkness helps very much indeed because the host-seeking free micro-organism is equipped with a food reserve of chlorophyl which it can't consume by photosynthesis unless there is light. So you can actually starve them.

If you want chemicals, and not the patented lines mentioned above, then use those suggested for white spot. Five hundred milligrams per gallon of Penbritten has been recommended by some: as have penicillin and streptomycin at 250 mg per gallon.

Or try 10 parts per million of acriflavine.

Ozonizers and ultra-violet ray lights are a great help. With many marines the anemones act as lice-removers, and pick the Oodinium spots off the fish – for example the Clown fishes from the West Indies, most Damsels and others.

A good old hit-and-miss method is suddenly to alter the temperature, the specific gravity, or both, on the theory that the fish will survive but the micro-organisms won't. Some people even plonk the fish in fresh water (!) for some 60 seconds, repeating the dose once a day for three days; some also combine this with a dose of copper sulphate of say 10 milligrams per gallon.

Benedenia This is a larger version of Oodinium and causes skin irritations so that the fish rubs itself against external objects.

Same treatment as for Oodinium, with the addition perhaps of streptomycin conjoined with penicillin, both of strength 250 milligrams per gallon.

People give fancy names to other diseases of both freshwater and marine fish. They are correct enough, but out-of-date in practice as new strains come in with new imports. The rate is such that any book would be obsolescent before even being printed; you'd need a daily news-sheet to keep up.

In these good old days of the pioneer you make your medicines as you go – with commonsense, and mixing intuitively. *Most fish do in fact survive!*

Useful hints of measurement
1 lb = 16 oz = 454 grams. 1 ounce = 28·4 grams.
1 kilogram = 1,000 grams = 2·2 lbs.
1 litre = 1,000 cubic centimetres. 1 gallon (Imperial) = 3·8 litres.
1 cubic foot of water weighs 62·4 lbs, and contains 7·5 gallons.
Length × width × height (in feet) × $6\frac{1}{4}$ = number of gallons.
1 acre of water (12″ deep) = 43,560 cubic feet = 326,000 gallons = 2,718,000 lbs.
1 gallon = 4 quarts = 8 pints = 3,800 cc; weighs 8·34 lbs or 3,800 grams.

Labeo erythruras. *Red-finned Shark.
6″. Thailand. Similar to the
Red-tailed Black Shark. Needs clean
bright algae-rich waters.*

143

CHAPTER 8
THE FISH

Popular scientific groupings have been observed, as have the accepted scientific names, for ease of international identification; also, every now and then a fish is examined in greater detail in an attempt to seek out its preferences of habitat (cf. beginning of chapter 7). The hope is that the aquarist at home will try the same method of intuitive understanding, and hence have happier fish; obviously, this is an approach of 'tomorrow, rather than of yesterday'. Fortunately, it has already caught on.

Characins An enormously widespread range found in the south of the North American continent and in South America, as well as in Africa. As you would expect they vary widely, but on the whole can make lovely aquarium fish, especially those found in rivulets and streams, rather than the main rivers.

Hence overgrowing vegetation, strong sunlight, soft water of low DH; constant variation from rain or season, and temperatures of around the 72°–80°F (22°–27°C) mark; feeding on all things including algae, even the carnivorous teeth-featured fish, who usually prefer insects to heavy dense lumps of flesh; often in shoals.

Please note that the vegetation should be sheltering *overhead*; the waters themselves being relatively clear, with only occasional clumps for protection.

For conditioning up to breeding pitch some live foods like daphnia or tubifex would of course be welcomed; so too would shredded or scraped beef, liver, fish, crab (no shell fragments please), white worms, garden worms, beef heart, etc. etc. Cooked foods are accepted too, so a scrap (washed), e.g. chicken, from your plate may be just right.

Breeding is easy as a rule, and is done in flocks, i.e. a number at a time. Prize breeding, or line breeding, is done with selected pairs; usually starting with a young group and allowing them to pair off. Viewed from above and looking from tail to head the female tends to bulge more, often on the left. The male is often larger, more pronounced coloration and finnage and has a hooked anal fin. Often slimmer. It is usual to condition up the parents separately, and to introduce the female first into the (sterilized?) tank, often at dusk, the male later, and with the hope of a spawning at dawn.

Many fish like slightly higher temperatures like 75°–82°F (24°–28°C); so, if in doubt, raise temperature a couple of degrees to encourage breeding.

The more clear-eyed the fish and the more its body sheen gleams, the less it stands dirt, and the longer its eggs take to hatch, say 48 hours instead of 36.

144   Spawning often scatters the eggs, most are semi-adhesive, and

Brackish-water fish

Right and below: Scatophagus argus.
10". Malaysia, Australia,
Pacific Islands. Many variations,
notably the red and the tiger scats,
also the green. Peaceful shoalers,
lively, always hungry. Live anywhere
with anyone, and can stand fantastic
water differences — from fresh,
brackish to full salt.
Their short barbles and over-eager
mouth indicate their greed;
their haphazard, blotched marks/dots
show that they can survive in
clear/cloudy/bright/murky conditions;
their circular laterally compressed bodies
proclaim their preference for deeper
waters; their trim finnage helps them
keep ever on-the-go.

Right: Monodactylus argenteus.
8". Malaysia, East Africa.
Silver-sheened, with gold fins, they have
similar hardy tolerances like the scats
except that their clear bright bodies
demand similar waters, aerated for
preference. Nomads, like the scats,
they yet appreciate the safety of a home,
e.g. a cave, rock-clefts, reed-like plant
thickets etc, from which to forage for
food. 78°–82°F (25°–28°C).

Tropical Marine fish

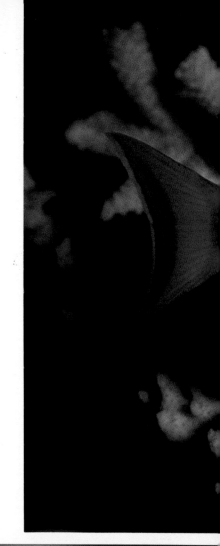

Right: Acanthurus leucosternon.
Surgeon. 7". Indian Ocean.
Pacific Ocean. Typical of fish having
extra sharp edges, spines and ridges in
the tail and dorsal fins which can cut'
viciously in defence. To soothe their
fear, have other fish in the tank first,
not the same size so as to be rival, but
either much smaller (no fear) or much
bigger (no need to 'prove themselves').
Algae: green foods like lettuce or
spinach, and a home of their own,
and all should be well. Beautiful blue!
Water 78°–82°F (25°–28°C).
Below: Amphiprion frenatus.
Clown fish. 6". East Indies, Africa.
Typical of this tomato-coloured group.
Likes to have anemones (to pick off its
Oodinium cysts). Needs coaxing
regarding food because it is easily
frightened. Prefers a shoal, provided its
own territory is safe. Likes algae.
Hardy. Females are thicker set,
with more rounded tail, the male tail
tending to extend at top or base, or both.
If gorged on the food the genital papillae
protrude, the male's are pointed,
the female's rounded. Spawning at
75°–80°F (24°–27°C).
Below right: Amphiprion polymnus.
4". Less often found than A. frenatus.
Lovely white head, back band,
and tomato nose. Hardy.

Overleaf: Balistoides niger.
Clown Trigger. 12". Pacific.
Gorgeous yellow mouth, round white
pebbles on its chocolate belly,
back flecked with gold, striking tail,
enormous head (with powerful teeth),
and its functional dorsal fin which has
three spines. A roofed cave of sufficient
size is essential. The fish darts rather
than swims. Not peaceful, it is
constantly nibbling for food, blowing jets
of water to flush out molluscs and
crustacea. It will shift aquarium
furnishings around – very powerful;
it will move/blow/bite really large
equipment or corals. Known to pick up
pieces and deliberately drop them on
other fish below.
Overleaf, inset: Apogon orbicularis.
The famous Cardinal. West Indies,
Florida. Nocturnal, as its subdued
(for marine) colours would suggest, but
becomes a day feeder in captivity. Very
hardy, it still needs the darkness of a cave
for shelter. In marine fish a bolt-upright
dorsal can indicate fright, but these
double dorsals are normally held high.

Above: Chaetodon lunula.
Butterfly Fish. 4″–8″. Pacific.
Typical of these well-loved favourites of
many colorations. Easily frightened,
and has to be encouraged to eat. A home
of its own is a must. The eye is
camouflaged and there is, as the
illustration shows, a prominent false
eye, which together combine to throw a
would-be attacker off aim as the fish
darts in an unexpected direction.

Right: Euxiphipops navarchus.
Angel Fish. 8″–12″. From the Pacific
and the Florida coasts, in many colours
and types. Sharp spikes on their gill
plates enable them to look after
themselves. Often confused with the
Butterfly Fish.

Below: Chaetodon kleini. *6″.*
West Indies, Florida. Another typical
example. Likes algae, live brine shrimps,
Norwegian shrimps, shredded beef,
scraped hearts, diced crab,
chopped spinach, lettuce, etc.

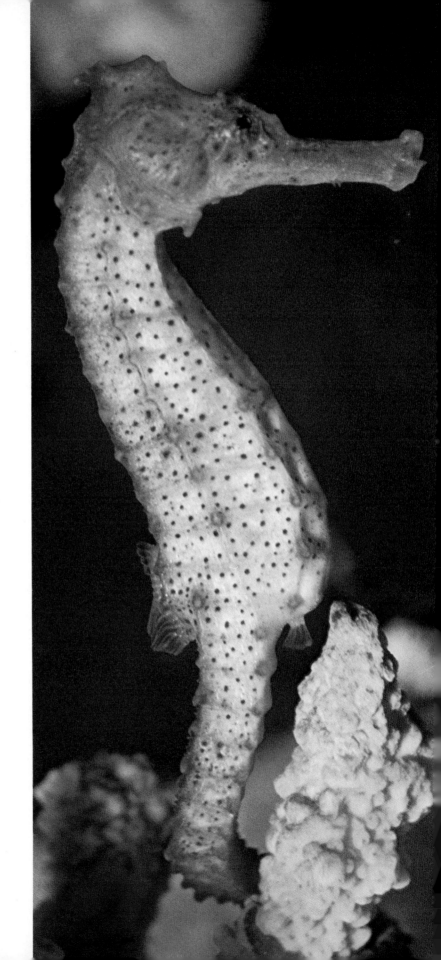

Left: Heniochus intermedius.
A Butterfly or an Angel?
The divisions overlap. 12".
Found everywhere on Indian Ocean
and Pacific coasts; hearty eater,
including algae, too busy eating to
quarrel provided it is left alone,
likes shoaling. Lovely flowing dorsal,
denoting defence, not attack. Tends to
wander, if the tank is big enough and
the other fish don't object. Should be fed
twice a day or more, not forgetting algae.

Left: Lutjanus sebae.
Emperor Snapper. Indo-Pacific.
Indicative of the many new varieties
coming along.
Should be treated like a Trigger Fish.

Right: Hippocampus kuda.
Sea Horse. 8". Florida. The good old
oldie that started the craze for marines,
now itself overshadowed by the new
brightly coloured varieties.
Cute prehensile tail for twining round
twigs, to perch on, so please provide
resting perches. The males carry the
eggs in their pouches. Peaceful and
hardy, their tiny mouths and slow
movements show that plentiful food
must go to them, not they to the food.
Other varieties exist, of course,
including the 2" Dwarf.

Above left: Paracanthurus hepatus.
[B]lue Surgeon. 9". Indo-Pacific.
[B]eautiful vivid blue, with bright yellow
[tai]l. Markings are defensive, so protect
[it] with a suitable home. So beautiful,
[ne]w variations keep coming so that the
[pr]oportion/shade of blue to yellow can
[alt]er quite widely.

[B]elow left: Naso lituratus.
[Gr]ey Surgeon. Indo-Pacific.
[A]nother relative newcomer showing
[th]e extension of the Surgeon family
[re]garding type and markings.
[Th]e mouth and tail are still precise.

Above: Pomacanthus imperator.
Emperor Angel. 12". Indian Ocean.
Gorgeous blue sheened body with bright
gold/yellow undulating lines, and tail.
Typical of the Angels; easily frightened
and made snappy, nearly always against
other Emperor Angels which are
regarded as rivals. One specimen alone
can easily be kept in a community.

155

Right: Pterois antennata.
Scorpion Fish or Lion Fish. 18".
Indian Ocean, Pacific Ocean.
Predatory, but not unduly vicious
or greedy, and will leave others alone
if really well fed and housed.
Poisonous spines – therefore thoroughly
protect it so that it does not have to
throw its weight around to assert its
territorial rights. Likes bright,
well-lit waters. Grows fast, as do most
ocean fish. Also can 'grunt' audibly like
the Triggers, and many other marines.
Said to like 72°–74°F (22°–23°C)
and pH 8·3–8·6.
Left: Pterois volitans. *Scorpion Fish.*
12". The most often found and
therefore kept, of this family.

Below: Rhineacanthus aculeatus.
Trigger Fish. 12". Hawaii and Africa.
Peaceful beauty. Note the typical erect
dorsal with which it can lock itself
into position, and the wonderfully
camouflaged mouth and eye.

Left: Zebrasoma veliferum. *Surgeon.*
18". Hawaii, Florida, South Africa.
Beautiful finnage. Must have rock clefts
and deep waters, otherwise it wilts quickly.
Dainty eater, tameable, likes algae.

Below: Scarus jonesi. *Parrot Fish.*
18". West Atlantic. Relatively new.
Not quite a typical Wrasse yet similar—
note the firm terminal mouth, clear eye,
and nocturnal or crepuscular colours.
Dim light and plenty of green foods are
needed. Peaceful, if well housed; does
not like being crowded. Hard working
and hungry, almost a scavenger. At
night it wedges itself into a rock cave,
as do the Triggers, and exudes a mucus
envelope to completely cover its body,
and effective protection against predators
who search for food by smell or sound.

Below left: Thalassoma lunare.
Wrasse. 8". Indian Ocean, Pacific
Ocean. Typical of these very active,
restless, hardy, ever-hungry beauties.
Must have a cave, an arch, a shell, a
cleft, etc. for a home. Hates the cold,
when it tends to bury itself in the sand;
likewise frightened or when first
introduced to the tank, if no sand is
available it lies on its side at the bottom.

Albino Moray eel. Typical of the many sea creatures that are too large for most home tanks.

Platax orbicularis. *Bat Fish. 18″.*
Indian Ocean, Pacific Ocean.
Perhaps the largest and the best of them all (except possibly the Modrish Idol which it resembles). A great favourite. Tameable, hardy, peaceful.
Grows quickly, and tends to lose its colours in small unsatisfactory tanks. Looks beautiful when happy, i.e. when well fed and housed. Likes deep waters and bright lights. Don't forget to feed algae.

Monodactylus sebae. *Unusual.
This fish is best in salt water; in fact
many claim it to be marine. Less hardy
than some.*

these have to be protected or they get eaten afterwards – plants, nylon mops, false bottoms to the tanks, crevices formed by marbles or largish pebbles, almost anything will do. The water need not be more than 8″–10″ deep for most Characins.

Unfertilized and diseased eggs add to the relatively-mastered hazards of hatching – draughts, hostile bacteria, etc, and a cover plus a dimming of the light (in the case of many an outright exclusion of light for five days), and a mild disinfectant like acriflavine, can help. As does aeration, and real cleanliness – some people sterilize everything first.

When free-swimming the fry should grow evenly or you are giving wrong foods – too big or too small – or dust, or draught, etc. Infusoria cultures, baby foods, brine shrimp eggs, and grindal worms will lead on to adult foods like daphnia and tubifex.

Transferring the fry to bigger quarters after 10–20 days is a must; the sooner and the bigger the better. Many increase the depth of the fry water an inch per week for the first month or so.

Cyprinidae The largest single family of freshwater fishes found almost everywhere, especially in North America, Africa, Asia, and Europe. It includes Barbs, Rasboras, Danios, and Minnows.

The famous Barbs are ubiquitous in the streams and rivulets of India, Malaysia, China, and elsewhere; they like fast-flowing, clear waters, plenty of vegetation, and are omnivorous so please don't forget their liking for green foods. Quick and playful, they are always on the go, to the irritation of the staid, and tire each other out if in groups of at least three (two is not enough), to the evident relief of the staid. Their greed is indicated by their barbels, and fin-nipping can usually be traced to insufficient feeding. Recently renamed *Capoeta*, *Puntius*, and *Barbodes* replacing the well-known *Barbus*.

As you would expect from such energy and food consumption, their excreta is heavy. Their home waters are free-flowing, so aeration and filtration are called for. Important.

Danios, mostly from India, are used to even shallower water, and can be spawned in only 4″; but prefer distinctly warmer waters – imagine the temperature of a shallow stream in the heat of the Indian sun. **161**

Restless wandering, far swimming, movements are natural
to them, rather than the frolics-in-one area of the Barbs. A long
tank suits them fine; they are most interested in the top few
inches, and hate surface scum.

Rasboras are halfway between the Barbs and Danios in
requirements, loving gentle rivulets in hot moist sunny Malaysia. Defensive shoaling is necessary for these beautiful and gentle
fish, as are green foods and cleanliness.

The Minnows like deeper, faster, clearer waters with plenty
of space and light – as distinct from heat. Some, like the White
Clowns, can stand surprising degrees of cold.

Coldwater fish Dropping rapidly in popularity due to the
greater variety and colouring of the tropicals and the marines,
they still have their place especially in the newly growing fashion
162 for *indoor* ponds (page 73).

Amphiprion tricinctus. 5″.
*Newer version, with typical white bands,
of the Clown Percula or Clown
Anemone Fish, as these are often called.
Hardy.*

However, the distinction between coldwater aquarium fish like Orandas, Telescopic-eyed Black Moors, Fantails, Veiltails, etc, and the large fast-growing, needing-masses-of-room-and-oxygen fish like goldfish is important. Vital in fact, particularly as too many (uninformed) people still talk of keeping goldfish in tanks.

Ignore this, and trouble is guaranteed to ensue.

Respect it, and the tank coldwater beauties will win your hearts, especially if your personal preference is for fish of 2″–4″ rather than the standard 1″–2″ of the tropicals.

Golden rule: for a tank, the fish body should be shorter, more rounded, with better finnage; for a pond (*lots* of room plus oxygen), fast-swimming slim torpedo shapes up to lengths of 14″ and more are acceptable.

Labyrinths A fascinating group that have an auxiliary breathing apparatus so that they gulp oxygen neat from the air, as humans do, as well as absorbing that dissolved in the water. Both systems have to be allowed to work; preventing such a fish from surfacing to breathe would kill it very quickly – many an 'unexplained' death is due to ignorance of this fact. For instance, if you took it home from the dealer and the carton was full of water with no layer of air inside, the fish would easily be suffocated before it reached your tank. Basically very hardy. Refer to the caption of the famous Siamese Fighter, the *Betta splendens*, as a typical example of the Afro-Asian beauties.

Live bearers The easiest of all freshwater tropicals to keep and to spawn, therefore tremendous favorites. The difficult business of looking after the eggs, hatching them, and nourishing the fry till they are safely free-swimming is all done by Mother Nature inside the female fish, which gives birth to live babies – from 40 to 200 – usually in bursts, spread over hours or even days. It is not unknown to have several spawnings from one fertilization.

Most will eat anything; all appreciate live foods, and special foods for babies are sold.

The males can be left in the tank, although they aren't any help; both parents may eat their fry unless these are protected by plant thickets, breeding traps, etc.

Any talk of 'my water doesn't suit such and such a live bearer' is usually directly traceable to the following:

(a) Wrong pH or DH. Most fish are very tolerant. pH 7·0 or DH 8 suits pretty well all; as does 76°–78°F (24°–26°C); big variations are possible.

(b) Urine or hostile nitrites in the water. Clean the tank, and the filter, part change the water, and watch the improvement.

(c) Too few or too many plants; not enough privacy; especially important for nervous types like the Mollies.

(d) Insufficient vegetarian diet; just meat or fish is not enough.

Sexing is extremely easy as the long pointed male anal fin is used as a gonopodium; often, too, as in the Swordtails, the bottom of the caudal fin elongates or thickens.

The gravid spot (near the female vent) gets bigger, and darker in colour, as gestation proceeds; usually 2–8 weeks, **163**

depending on fish and on season. Her anal fin is short and rounded.

Many crosses with 'cousin fish' are possible, e.g. Swordtails with Platies. Beautiful are the variations, especially in tails and fins.

Cichlids These have long been 'out in the cold' because they were pugnacious and too big; with a few notable exceptions like the Angel fish whose grace and beauty conquered all prejudice.

Enormous varieties, hence also of temperaments and of size, exist; but the detailed information on Discus could be a helpful guide to Cichlid preferences as these come increasingly into popular favour due to two main factors:

1. Aquarists often have more than one tank, and can now allocate one to Cichlids.

2. Tanks in general are increasing in size with the develop-

Ostracion tuberculatus.
Box, or Trunk, Fish. 14″. Indian Ocean, Pacific. Protect themselves by emitting a cloud of poison; in the aquarium this will kill everything including the Trunk Fish. Their flesh is 'poisonous' and other fish leave them alone.

ment of new rubber sealing techniques.

Egg-laying Tooth Carps These 'killie' fish have such beauty and accentuated colouring – not to mention finnage – that they have more devoted (even fanatical) adherents.

Deservedly popular, especially for the small tank.

Catfish and Loaches Nature's scavengers. Peaceful, hardworking, clearing up the mess that others leave; not only getting no thanks for it, but even sometimes being blamed for 'stirring up the bottom'!

Their bodies proclaim their (modest) preferences as stated on page 134. For heating the bottom 1″ of the tank see page 37. The more dark and blotchy the body marking the more muck they can stand – although they would prefer less. Clearer markings obviously require clearer waters.

Like the Labyrinths, they have the auxiliary breathing apparatus, and must gulp neat air fairly frequently; taken home **165**

Dascyllus aruanus. *Damsel.*
$4\frac{1}{4}''$. Red Sea, Florida, Australia.
Typical of the Damsels. Subdued
colours demand half or oblique light.
Nervous in the open – it needs a dark
cave. Hardy, eats anything. Will shoal,
once its home is safe. Likes anemones to
clean up its skin.

imprisoned in a container completely full of water and void of free air, they may be dead on arrival – suffocated.

Hardy; they will stand most water and eat most foods. Being bottom dwellers they prefer lower temperatures of 70°–74°F (21°–24°C). Often allergic to salt. pH 7·2.

Sexing is difficult, but breeding is easy, often spread over 2–4 days, hatching in 3–6 days. Dimmer shaded areas with a few brighter patches are inducive to spawning, of course, and smooth rocks are liked.

Miscellaneous For the pond, a few are illustrated as indicative of those you might like to keep in your indoor pond, left unheated.

But what is to stop you, indoors, from experimenting with easy-to-fix heaters, and hence a whole new range of fish and plants?

Brackish water fish Very many kinds exist, including the *Toxotes jaculator* already described. They live basically where the river meets the sea, and their eager search for food carries them into salty waters. They can be kept in either, but take on clearer or heightened colouring in brackish water, and better still in sea water when the best comes into bloom. The flow of the river is still appreciable at the delta so that aerated waters help, although these eager eaters can stand surprising variations. Their changes of colour are so varied, that you can sometimes doubt if it's the same fish.

They love, and need, the protection of a shoal as they are nomads, driven by hunger. If cornered (as in an aquarium) they huddle for protection and take cover if possible – in plants, caves, or rocks. Recovering their confidence they venture out (for food!) but dash back if disturbed. The eggs are free-scattered. Live foods especially liked. Usually only 2″–5″ sizes are found in the aquarium. 75°–84°F (24°–28°C), pH 7·0–8·2, DH 6–14.

Tropical marines As far as tropical marines are concerned these are the good old days of the individual pioneer, when much has still to be learnt; just as it was for freshwater tropicals in the 1920s. However, it seems more than likely that, at the end of the 1970s, marines will have replaced freshwater tropicals. First, because they are beautiful; second, because they *do* survive. Healthy fish usually have plenty of flesh around the abdomen. Invertebrates like a higher specific gravity of say 1·028, whereas many fish seem best in 1·023 or even 1·021. The pH seems best around 8·2 or 8·3, although natural seawater varies from 7·8 to 8·9.

A healthy anemone tends to have sticky stems as well as sticky tentacles; when alarmed it contracts strongly retracting the tentacles and 'drawing in' tightly into its central mouth; if the water is beginning to foul it does the reverse and regurgitates its stomach in protest, ejecting out refuse and refuse balls.

If a fish is too large to be accommodated within the diameter of an anemone, then the tentacles may be used to sting in self-defence; so please keep size in mind. Of course, some anemones are nocturnal, and remain 'closed' by day.

Our classification is the simple one of well-known types **167** denoted by scientific names; all could be kept by you in your tank, if you follow the guidance of earlier chapters. Please remember the golden rule; you buy an extra filter *before* you buy that extra fish.

Marine communities Fear is ever present in life, and the marine world is no exception. Although the ocean is vast any section of it is likely to contain a mixture – hence a balance – of many types, some apparently hostile to each other, yet all contributing to the harmony of the whole. Hence, all will live with all, provided fear is not unduly aroused – when all will turn on all. The more similar the colouring and size, the more likely the attack.

Ways of mitigating rivalry have already been stressed; unequal sizes together, not two of the same species (unless they are shoal lovers), clear demarcation lines, enough room, food, and shelter, and, most important, the simultaneous introduction of all the fish into the tank, already rich in algae.

Bearing in mind the guidelines, the choice and scope are yours. There are no absolute rules, so why not experiment? You should only be careful not to overcrowd, having less than half the number you might have in a freshwater tropical tank, and provided that the rate of filter flow is 100–150 gallons per hour.

Here are several suggested marine communities, intended only as a rough guide. Each of the 'main' fish are readily interchangeable with others, but the suggestions would serve as a basis for proportion.

Community A – for tank of any reasonable size with filter flow of 100–150 gallons per hour.
1 *Chaetodon lunula* Butterfly Fish. Medium size.
4 Damsels (*Dascyllus*) of unequal size and different types. Smallish
4 Clowns (*Amphiprion*) of unequal size and different types. Smallish
Possible additions, if enough room and enough *extra filters*.
1 *Heniochus intermedius*. Medium
1 *Paracanthurus hepatus* Blue Surgeon. Medium
1 *Platax orbicularis* Bat Fish. Small (it grows fast!)
Also useful would be anemones, shrimps, crabs, and molluscs, as scavengers (hermit crabs have been known to escape from uncovered tanks!). Other scavengers which are often kept are spiny urchins, brittle stars (from the North American coasts), small starfish, and coral shrimps. It rather depends on who eats whom! A hint about crustacea, as mentioned before – they must be removed *before* they start to decompose!

Community B – 30-gallon tank, filter flow 100–150 gallons p/hr.
1 *Amphiprion percula*
1 *A. tomato*
2 *A. polymnus*
2 *Abudefduf coeruleus* Blue Demoiselle
2 *Dascyllus trimaculatus* Domino types
1 main black or dark coloured fish. Medium size (about 4″)
1 main yellow fish, e.g. *honey gregorys*.
Neon Gobies *Elacatinus oceanops* as scavengers and delousers

Pterois volitans. *Scorpion Fish. Another photograph of this popular fish, illustrated in colour on page 156.*

are often recommended, say two for the above selection in place of the Dominoes.

Community C – 30-gallon tank, usual filter flow.
1 Yellow Wrasse   6″
1 Yellow-tailed Damsel   2″
1 Percula Clown   3″
1 hermit crab   1″
1 *Euxiphipops navarchus*   3″
1 Neon Goby   3″
1 French Angel   2″
1 *Dascyllus*   2″

For an experiment you could also add 1 Butterfly (3″) if you could persuade it to feed with all the rest.

Community D – invertebrates only. 15-gallon tank, usual filter flow.
1 hermit crab
1 coral shrimp
1 anemone   3″
1 starfish
1 brittle star
1 sea urchin
1 arrow crab

Feeding could be on live brine shrimp, chopped shrimp, Norwegian brine shrimp, freeze-dried foods, chopped fish (not oily ones), algae.

Community E – 5-gallon tank, suggested sp. gr. 1·022–1·025
3 hermit crabs
2 small crabs
6 *Dwarf* Sea Horses

Alternative method of introduction It has been stressed that, when establishing a community, all the fish must be introduced simultaneously. However one can try an alternative method as follows.

Put in, first, 4 Damsels only, and leave for three months – partly for you to get accustomed to the painstaking daily feeding and siphoning, and partly to allow the high level of ammonia and of nitrites to fall, and most especially to allow the green algae to develop in profusion (encouraged by special lights). Nitrites result from urine, and from bacteria following the introduction of food, the tiniest fragments of which start to decompose; meanwhile helpful nitrates are 'maturing' as the undergravel filter works and finally these 'overcome' the nitrites and the danger level falls.

With this method of 'maturing', it is suggested that any ozonization should be kept off the bottom one inch of water so as not to destroy the helpful nitrates in the undergravel filter. Remember the rate of flow is 100 gallons per hour, or more; some aquarists also ask that the undergravel filter covers the entire floor and has such a strong 'grip' at the periphery that no water can seep in except through its main filter area.

Then, after the three months, the main fish like Surgeons, Angels, or Butterfly can be introduced simultaneously, and of big enough size (say 3″) not to be attacked by the Damsels.   **171**

About the author

Reginald Dutta first started keeping fish, including marine specimens, in 1937 after graduating from London University, and is now the Managing Director of Fish Tanks Ltd, the oldest established fish specialists in London's West End.

As such he writes from within the very heart of this fast changing industry with a lifetime's working experience behind him.

His fame as a 'fish doctor' has gained him an international clientele, including the Royalty of several nations, the distinguished and the famous at Court, the professions, industry and entertainment.

He pioneered the insistence on the internal beauty of tank layout, and his designs have long been trend setters.

The advice he offers is practical, workable, and is aimed to make the fish happy – a point that rates very high. His advice will also save you expense, help you to avoid unnecessary mistakes, and will keep your tank up-to-date.

Flying Saucers are the author's other interest, and his book *Flying Saucer Viewpoint* (Pelham Books, 52 Bedford Square, London WC1) has set tongues wagging in 'this village planet earth'; so much so that a sequel has been evoked, *Flying Saucer Message* from the same publisher, which seeks to go beyond just 'nuts and bolts', to grow in deeper understanding.

Other books by Reginald Dutta
Beginner's Guide to Tropical Fish (*Pelham*)
Manual for Fish Tank Owners (*Pelham*)
Encyclopaedia of Tropical Fish (*Pelham*)
Tropical Fish and Fish Tanks (*Collins*)
Right Way to Keep Pet Fish (*Hutchinson*)

Under the name his friends call him, Rex Dutta
Flying Saucer Viewpoint (*Pelham*)
Flying Saucer Message (*Pelham*)

175